I0449060

Radical Psychological Modes
&
Suicides

by

Patty R. Gradsky

Copyright © 2019 by Patty R. Gradsky.

ISBN: Softcover   978-1-4500-2700-7
               eBook   978-1-7960-4132-3

All rights reserved. No part of this book may be reproduced or transmitted in any form or by any means, electronic or mechanical, including photocopying, recording, or by any information storage and retrieval system, without permission in writing from the copyright owner.

Scripture quotations marked NKJV are taken from the New King James Version. Copyright © 1982 by Thomas Nelson, Inc. Used by permission. All rights reserved.

Print information available on the last page.

To order additional copies of this book, contact:
Xlibris
1-888-795-4274
www.Xlibris.com
Orders@Xlibris.com
55176

SUICIDE NOTES
In the making . . .

1. Loss of hope, faith; a feeling of impending, inevitable doom.

2. Ongoing depression which can lead to despair.

3. Major loss (ex: divorce, a death, job, financial, emotional bankruptcy.

4. Extreme behavior to "numb down" reality: abuse of drugs, alcohol, food, sleep—even the computer. (are examples)

5. Trouble recognizing "self-worth", or "love".

6. Suicidal impulses acted-on more than once before.

7. Afflicted with self-sorrow, narcissism to some extent.

8. Suffering with a serious illness—physical or mental.

9. A disconnect—isolated.

10. Talks about suicide—fits the profile before "actual suicide note."

The spirit of suicide is a hooded beast on horseback, hell-bent-at-break-neck-speed to take your breath away and to trample it into the dust.

Dedicated to

Mrs. Waneta E. Dillingham
spiritual intercessor, encourager, friend and aunt.

God is the Father of mercies who inspires us to encourage others with same affliction.

CONTENTS

INTRODUCTION

I felt compelled to write about suicide as the second book in the "Radical Psychological Moods" bipolar series. I was plagued with the mercurial-mood-shifts of manic depressive-bipolar disorder, and have experienced suicidal thoughts, impulses and attempts in the past.

Suicide is no longer on my mind, and it's "not the way to go." Suicide is, however, in my mind to raise consciousness, sound the alarm, ring a bell that resonates with and quickens the inner spirit to push back the enemy. The wolf is at the door, huffing and puffing, threatening to "blow you away."

You have a right and a responsibility to defend and protect your God given life. Something that resonates with me is from the pages of, My Utmost For His Highest, a Daily Devotional, by Oswald Chambers:

" . . . God does not give us overcoming life: He gives us life as we overcome." Going back to the beginning is a good place to start. All the way back to, "In the beginning God created the heaven and the earth". Genesis 1:1. God is the ultimate source—to my mind—of all things, and what limited knowledge and perspectives that I bring to this book falls far short. His omnipotence in all matters, including "bipolar and unstable minds and suicide", transcends any utmost insight I might have. Such as it is, however, it corresponds as "inside source" from the mind of an individual who has lived with bipolar disorder and suicidal thoughts.

For those who haven't read, Radical Psychological Mood Shifts, I will go back and give you some background and quotes to bring you up to date. From Chapter Two: "I Thought The Pavement Was The Sky: "Bipolar means two opposite poles: mania and depression. What are the symptoms? Was my behavior indicative of a neurotic personality, or was I merely insane ? I was too embedded into my own psychosis to view it objectively. I believed that I just had an artist's temperament, and that was just me. Creative types were supposed to be rebels, a little dark, a little "mad", weren't they? . . . I was hospitalized the first time when I was in my early twenties. I was admitted for attempted suicide. A police officer was required to put it on record, and stood by while my stomach was pumped. It's against the law to take your own life, and if you survive, are automatically committed to a psychiatric institution . . . for someone who wasn't rational, I rationalized a lot. Is insanity an acquired taste? Maybe I started out on my neural pathways headed in the right direction, but I developed irrational pasterns of thinking and behaving . . .

I became an edge walker. I took scary, bizarre, and unhealthy risks, I would "cross over", almost defiantly, into other camps, other strata, other friction, like a rogue dog, to sniff and run before I'm dead meat in someone's stew. I was a "tar baby". That's someone who trouble sticks to. All they know is hurt and be hurt . . .

I was a rapid cycler. My highs could last for a few hours, days or weeks, then I would crash into that long a period of depression. It was a continual struggle to try and integrate these two opposite personalities into some kind of manageable identity."

During that period, I was told by doctors, psychiatrists, psychologists, hospitals and clinics, that I would "be on medication the rest of my life." Quoting again: "During the lucid periods I seemed to act as a referee. I was quiet, in a watchful state, because I couldn't let down my guard. At any given moment, one of us would be hurling around the corner to take its turn at the wheel. I couldn't relax, but to those around me, I appeared mellow, and laid-back. This illusion could be quickly blown away, however, if anyone inadvertently touched me, or became verbally aggressive, challenging me . . .

Another characteristic or symptom of manic depression or bipolar is grandiose feelings. There's a fine line here, or distinction, in some instances. A lot of the time when I would shoot for the moon and the stars, my exuberance translated into a shooting star—brilliant, and colorful, but quickly spent, falling to earth like a child's sparkler. But now and then my high-minded goals coincided with its success.

What I wrote about in, Radical Psychological Mood Shifts, was the truth. That was information on bipolar disorder, and my personal thoughts, feelings and experiences. In that book, I go into symptoms and treatments, as I found them to be. The doctors and nurses said that I would be on medication for the rest of my life. And I was—for a considerable number of years. If anyone needed something to stop or even slow down the roller coaster madness of bipolar-manic depression—it was me.

The years following diagnosis and treatment and wanting to write about bipolar illness, was also a time of turning back to God. It took more than a wrong turn or two to get as lost as I was in mind and spirit.

I had admitted that I was sick mentally, emotionally and spiritually, and I made that first phone call for help that began the journey. The "meds" upheld a much needed truce in my warring brain in order for God and me to "re-negotiate the peace." The reality of my unstable mind was self-defeating. I once told my daughter that, "Being in a bipolar mind was like trying to thread a needle while riding a roller coaster".

With all that said, it's up to us to deal with what's happening, not how the psychiatrist, the pharmacist, professional, and friends deal with how we're dealing with it. It's our mind and body, and relief from symptoms is real, but do some monitoring of your own. On the bright side, it's not impossible that symptoms could abate after a substantial period of treatment.

I know that I "could have been on 'meds' for the rest of my life", but that didn't happen. What has happened is that I didn't give up hope that faith in God and new behavior can become template overlays that dominate.

Chapter Five, from, Radical Psychological Mood Shifts, "Suicide—Not The Way To Go", is reprinted as PART ONE, of the First Chapter in this book: Radical Psychological Moods Dark Fall / Bipolar and Unstable Minds and Suicide. This book is about self-killing from different perspectives and different ways to, "not go there". All of the information and perspectives that I present, and how anyone may interpret it is individual, and should not be read in exclusion of professional, mental health counsel.

If you picked up this book because "suicide is on your mind," I want to remind you of one thing—you're looking into a dark pool of thoughts that don't reflect a true image of yourself. With that thought in mind, go and talk to a friend, or pastor, or someone in your family who you like and trust, but go see a mental health professional right away. Get help, and "ride it out"—let the death-wish-mood "pass"—not you.

Mankind gravitates to cycles of opposing forces. He rises and falls from dark despair, swaying on the edge of his destruction, to escalating and sublime reaches of heaven . . .

. . . AND WHEN HE COULD LAUGH AT THE RAGE OF HIS VANITIES—HE FELL STILL.

Chapter One

Suicide—Not The Way To Go

"I didn't want to die. I just wanted to end my pain.". Attempted suicides say this. I've said it.

PART ONE: Chapter Five Reprint from—*RADICAL PSYCHOLOGICAL MOOD SHIFTS*: "Suicide—Not The Way To Go"

I've attempted suicide several times on my life. My death wish persisted off and on for years. I held onto the idea and thoughts of suicide, and considered it an ongoing option. It was strangely comforting. I held onto the idea like a comfort blanket that I eventually kicked to the floor.

At one of those periods, I wrote this poem:

Suicide

I held it close
to my heart,
like a brown
fuzzy, teddy bear.
All through the dark
hours of the night
I clutched its presence.
A voice within
begged me to
toss it to the floor,
but I held on
for dear life.

I found a support group for bipolar and depressives that I went to on Friday evenings at a local hospital. The educational meeting was led by a doctor who was also bipolar and had been level on lithium for over twenty years. The program had a rotating lecture series that I attended for several years.

Hurting people wanting answers. The Friday night sessions were nearly always full. At the end of the two and a half hours we had what was called by Dr. Sam, a "check-in" time. This last thirty minutes was reserved for us to say whatever was on our minds—if we chose to.

One evening at check-in, a newcomer, a lawyer, needed to talk. Paraphrased, this is what he had on his mind:

> "My life got way out of hand. I was cycling every two or three weeks. I stayed up working for days and nights until I collapsed from exhaustion.
>
> I was promiscuous, overbearing, belligerent and agitated. Then the bottom would drop out, and I'd go down for the count. My life was hopeless. I wanted to kill myself, and I planned a way to do it. Then, all of a sudden, I'd be up and running, the depression forgotten. I could do no wrong; I was king of the mole hill, and I plotted money-making schemes constantly.
>
> I went to the bank and withdrew 20,000 dollars—all my savings—and gave it to this guy I met in a bar. He had this great idea involving boats that would make us rich. Of course, I never saw the man again—or the money. That was the last straw. I was going for help. But, I never did. The next time the depression hit, I was seriously suicidal. I took my .38 pistol and went for a ride around midnight. I drove for hours, and ended up way out in the country. I pulled off this two-lane onto a dirt road.
>
> I parked the car by a stand of trees, and sat there in the dark. I began to drink the whiskey I'd brought. I'd told myself that when the bottle was empty, I'd blow my brains out.
>
> Well, about that time, I felt someone else's gun at my head, and a man's voice, "Give me your money, man, or I'll pull the trigger!"
>
> As calm as could be, I turned my head to look at him, and said, "Go ahead, man, you'll save me the trouble." "I'm not kidding, I'll blow your head off! Hand over your wallet, m—F—!"
>
> I became instantly enraged. I jumped out of the car, almost knocking him down with the car door, and screamed in his face:

"Kill me! You f—! Then I started laughing and crying at the same time. I was hysterical, a raving lunatic. That guy forgot all about robbing me, and took off running. All of a sudden, I thought that was very funny, and I quit crying, and laughed my head off instead of blowing my head off. I didn't want to end my life anymore. That day I saw a doctor. I was diagnosed a bipolar, manic depressive, and began medication. My doctor (pointing to our doctor/lecturer) said to come to the meeting tonight, that it's part of the treatment."

Soon after being stabilized on lithium, "Dan" was able to go back to being a practicing attorney, as he told us at a check-in one Friday evening.

For a bipolar, getting our balance is the tricky part. We have a penchant for extremes. It reminds me of a scene in an old western movie. This cowboy took a run at his horse to leap up and land astride the horse's back—only to fall off on the other side. The cowboy gets up, dusts himself off, and tries again, but lands on the ground on the other side of his horse where he started. Back and forth and back and forth, and so forth. I watched fascinated at the images on the screen very much like the extreme moods I experienced later in my life.

It's not easy to stay in balance and to stay centered for a bipolar. It's the lopsided, radical extremes of mood that rise and fall. The dark side of the fall is the black depression. Suicide happens when nothing breaks that free-fall but death itself.

CHAPTER FIVE—"Suicide—Not The Way To Go"
(From the 1st book: *Radical Psychological Mood Shifts*)

When I was correctly diagnosed with manic depression, or bipolar disorder, and began a prescribed drug treatment, along with psychotherapy over twelve years ago, I haven't considered suicide anymore, but for what it is: A KILLER. The suicidal thoughts that resulted in attempts, spanned two decades. During those approximately twenty years, there were three instances of attempts.

One of those points of despair was when I was in my early twenties. I was admitted to the E.R. For a drug overdose. A married Christian couple that were friends of mine, stayed at the hospital while the doctors worked to save the life I wanted to end.

I am grateful that they cared to be there, and to pray for me. The doctor came out into the hallway where my friends were waiting for word about me, and told them: Patty has a fifty-fifty chance of surviving . . . if she makes it through the next hour."

The doctor went on to inform them that there was a chance that I'd go into convulsions, and there could be possible brain damage. I'm grateful to God that neither happened.

Attempted suicides are said to be a cry for help. Everyone knows the story about the little lad who cried "wolf," one too many times. The first time he was believed, and the people came running. The second time, he got the same results. I think it was his third cry for help that everyone turned their backs on him. And that was the one time that the wolf ate him.

Statistics would call the lad a "completer." All "completers" usually attempt more than one suicide. The more attempts or threats, increases the danger of death by suicide.

Who is at risk? Teens, the elderly, men and women. The newspapers, magazine articles, and television., report that suicides among adolescents are escalating.

The taking of one's life can happen less dramatically, too. What about the ones that are destroying themselves slowly, or the "accidents." I knew a lady that had liver disease, and was warned by her physician to stop drinking alcohol. She kept right on, and eventually that wild turkey came home to roost on her tombstone. Maybe you've seen anorectic girls on some talk show on television. They were literally starving themselves to death. I recall that one of the girls had died, as later reported on an update. And other types of "accidental" deaths can come about by mixing alcohol and drugs, even prescription drugs.

Sexual abuse in childhood is the major cause of young girls becoming suicidal. One study on teen-age suicide indicated that one-third who had attempted suicide had been molested by some member of the family. And this statistic "after the fact": Out of two hundred young people who attempt, one succeeds; of every five who kill themselves, four have made at least one previous attempt. Even though most teens who threaten suicide give some warning beforehand, those close to them may not realize it until after.*

What pushes people to the edge ? What are the warning signs ? People who have a clinical or reactive depression, or who are bipolar and in a depression, are at risk. Suicidal feelings can, for the most part, be prevented by staying on prescribed medication, and staying off street drugs and alcohol. Our doctor advised us, that if in a crisis, contract with a friend until it passes.

Depression, a feeling of lost hope, of lost personal worth, an inability to cope with life events, can lead to suicidal thoughts. Ongoing stress, whether from a mental or physical disability can bring on frustration and depression that are potentials for considering suicide. Death can be surreal, especially to teen-agers, and impressionable people who take to heart the hard-rock lyrics that glorify suicide, and they become "completers."

It's an idea they want to emulate when movie or rock-star idols overdose, or die by more violent means. It's mostly young people who carry out a suicidal pact, the romantic aura of Romeo and Juliet. Somehow, it's not real to them. People who are suicidal, feel there's no way out for them, that there's a dead-end in the road, and they're out of gas. Maybe they can't communicate with their family, or they don't have a friend to turn to.

On the Oprah Show, a young woman told of losing her job, and living in her car. Things got worse, and she sold the car, and began living in the park. She used some of the money from the sale of the car to pay off a few debts. People told her to keep the money for herself until she got back on her feet, but she said they needed to be paid. She couldn't find a job, and continued to live in the park. The horror of hr life became a horrible tragedy. I learned that she hanged herself from a tree in that park.

Suicide was openly, sometimes tentatively, discussed in the group sessions. Many of us had first-hand experience, if not ourselves, then a friend, a family member, or a significant other. A mate speaks out, and tells the group that, "He's drinking too much, and says off by himself all day." Another lady confided, "If only he could sleep better at night . . . and eat. Sometimes he has crying spells . . ." Later that year her husband was hospitalized for an attempted suicide. If a member of the group said they were worried that a friend might be suicidal, someone always asked, "Are they giving their things away?" This is usually a sign that the person is thinking in that direction if other symptoms of depression are present. The person gives away their possessions because they feel that they won't need them anymore. The girlfriend of a college student who was bipolar, who'd had a previous suicide attempt, was frightened for him. She'd say, "He's too calm. Last week he was angry and blowing-up at me all the time."

While it's true that most people who have a plan to end their lives appear calm and even happy, it wasn't the case with her boyfriend. The story came out, that he had stopped taking his "meds." His mother, a PhD, and herself a bipolar, manic depressive, took her son to see a psychiatrist. The boyfriend's calm demeanor was due to his being stable on medication.

Calm is good, but the huge change in behavior from violent outbursts to cheerful serenity can be a warning sign of suicide. Once that decision has been made to "end their worries." they can appear to be on good terms with the world, and quite pleased with themselves.

Whenever there's a major loss, like the death of a loved one, or losing a job, or breaking-up with a mate, all can be potential risks for suicide, especially if drinking alcohol is overused to ease the pain. The alcohol is in itself a depressant, and the low feelings are magnified. Alcohol is known to lessen good judgment, and makes impulsive behavior more likely. Suicide has been called a final solution for a temporary problem. If suicidal thoughts happen, especially in a deep depression it's crucial to get help, to stay on medication.

When I'm in a low stretch of road, I think of how a scared kitten would feel in a deep, dark well, feeling he can't get out, and even if he could, what would be the point ? A despair so deep, he can't see beyond his whiskers. I can use a metaphor like that now, because that was how I felt—a long time ago. I like to think of myself as a lion now, more bold and less fearful of life; although, to be honest, I'm a pitiful lion at times, much akin to Dorothy's friend. To get my courage back, however, I sought out a power that is above all. I explain how that works for me in Chapter Nine, "Driving Up To Jerusalem."

In every town, there's usually one suicide prevention organization that offers an emergency hot-line. It was brought to my attention recently by someone who'd overdosed at a motel, and called his brother, that another source can be used. His brother called 911 and saved his life.

Thoughts of ending one's life can be overcome. If drugs like cocaine, and alcohol are overused, the depression can be a risk for suicide. An intervention by someone trusted, and counseling is needed to persuade them to get treatment. If counseling and medication are ministered, the suicidal mood will likely pass. It's helping that person to see better roads, to detour that dead-end he's focused on. If they continue to talk about suicide, take them to a hospital or a doctor, as quickly as possible.

Getting involved in a crisis center, or a suicide prevention program could make a big difference by teaching skills to suicidal people on how to dodge that final straw-man.

Road Tip: There's a KILLER on the highway, wearing an old T-Shirt with lyrics from a song, "Suicide Is Painless". DON'T PICK UP THAT HITCH-HIKER!

(Conclusion of Chapter Five from *Radical Psychological Mood Shifts*)

PART TWO: A "HISTORY" OF SUICIDE

Bipolar and unstable minds enjoy believing that we can "fix the problem even if it's wrong." A doctor will sometimes ask, "Where does it hurt?" The pain was too indescribable, so my solution was to "throw the baby out with the bathwater". Suicide, to my way of thinking now, is like destroying an entire kingdom to rid it of a dragon.

The dragon isn't the real you; it's a big lie, a deception that the real Dragon—Satan—is perpetrating on people. Of course we are culpable, like our first parents were. Yet, there was a diabolic persuasion that took place. The lie, however, caused the death of Adam and Eve. We don't have to take the bait—to take that first bite of the apple. Slaying the "dragon" (within) is as old as sin.

So, be kind to yourself. The "self" doesn't want to die yet. Because life will eventually come to an end—unless you're caught-up in the "rapture". "For the living know that they will die, but the dead know nothing, and they have no more reward here, for the memory of them is forgotten. Ecclesiastes 9:5.

Because God created Adam and Eve, not R2D2, (robot in Star Wars) you and I have choices, a free will. Suicide, I realize "after the fact", is a very cold-blooded "kill", carried out on "self" by an unstable, dark-side of a small part of the ego-brain where vanities raged and roared. It echoes the lies, the illusions and delusions brought down on all humanity by the most prideful and vain of all creatures. Once an exalted angel, Lucifer allowed pride and vanity to disfigure him into the darkest face of evil-pitted—pockets of hell, roaring like a lion walking about, seeking whom he may devour.

Lucifer's fall from Heaven thundered downward to earth to impact like a bolt of lightening discharging his prior image to become the father of lies and murder; not archangel, but our arch enemy, Satan—the creation of his own vanities.

Lucifer's H-Bombshell-explosion of destruction and unspeakable, dark evil created a cloud over the world that reached to Heaven, and like a nuclear fall-out, contaminated the human family to this very present day.

"And there was war in heaven; Michael and his angels fought against the dragon; and the dragon fought and his angels, and prevailed not; neither was their place found anymore in heaven. And the great dragon was cast out, that old serpent, called the Devil, and Satan, that deceived the whole world: he was cast out into the earth, and his angels were cast out with him."

Revelation 12:7-9

The seed of the spirit of suicide was planted in the beginning—in the Garden of Eden. It would reap sorrow and destruction and death for all generations. And the war rages on: "For we wrestle not against flesh and blood, but against principalities, against powers, against the rulers of the darkness of this world, against spiritual wickedness in high places." Ephesians 6: 12. Lucifer's "creation of vanities" and his downfall was ultimately passed down to mankind and can be found in—

"The Seven Deadly Sins":

1. PRIDE—is the excessive focus on ones own self aggrandizement that interferes with a recognition of the grace of God. Pride is also known as *vanity*.
2. ENVY—is the desire for others' traits, states, abilities or situation.
3. GLUTTONY—is an inordinate desire to consume more than what one requires.
4. LUST—is an excessive craving for the pleasures of the body.
5. ANGER—is an individual inclined toward resentment and wrath.
6. GREED—is the desire for material wealth or gain, ignoring the realm of the spiritual. It means to covet.
7. SLOTH—is being idle and non-productive.

Of all the sins, PRIDE is at the top of almost every list. Known as the original sin and the most serious of the seven deadly sins, and the source of the other six. Basically it is the love of self to excess, especially in irreverence to God. In Dante's epic poem, the Divine Comedy, Dante's definition was: "love of self, perverted to hatred and contempt for one's neighbor."

Pride was what caused the downfall of Lucifer from heaven, and to become the devil himself, Satan. Vanity and narcissism are the biggest examples of the sin of pride. In the Divine Comedy, the contrite were made to walk with stone slabs tied to their backs to produce feelings of humility.

PROVERBS 6:16-19: There are six things the Lord hates, seven that are detestable to Him: 1.) haughty eyes 2.) lying tongue 3.) hands that shed innocent blood 4.) a heart that devises wicked schemes 5.) feet that are quick to rush into evil 6.) a false witness who pours out lies, and 7.) a man who stirs up dissension among his brothers". In general, however, most people think of the "so called seven deadly sins" as 1) pride, 2.) envy 3.) gluttony 4.) lust 5.) anger 6.) greed 7.) sloth. But it can be said that almost every sin under the sun could be listed under these categories.

The concept and tradition of the list in the Christian faith was originally organized by Pope Gregory Ist in the year 600. He also compiled the traditional list of virtues: faith, hope, charity, justice, prudence, fortitude, and temperance. As a "list," per se, the Bible does not refer these sins or virtues specifically in a named list. Without question the scriptures confirm and give evidence of "where and how" the seven deadly sins were made known.

In fact, the Bible has very little written about the subject of the sin of suicide itself. It could be because it didn't occur that often, and even imminent texts on death and the Bible give only a passing reference.

The subject of suicide in the Christian community isn't one they discuss much—to condemn or to condone, so as to appear unwilling to pass moral judgment, and care not to be responsible. So, the serious issue of suicide is for the most part overlooked.

We aren't lacking, however, in what the Christian view is, and what the scriptures (Bible) say. Five people are recorded in the Bible as having committed suicide. Saul and Judas, are two generally known names. Another person in the Bible who is widely known about is Samson. It's argued that Samson was a suicide (Judges 16: 26-31) The opposing view is that his intention was to bring down death to the Philistines, not to kill himself.

"Thou shalt not kill (murder)" is, of course, one of the Ten Commandments in the Bible. (the 6th) Suicide is self-murder. A strong piece of admonition in Ecclesiastes 7:17: "Don't be a fool—why die before your time?"

King David in the Old Testament, was so depressed that he wished that he'd never been born. "How long must I lay up cares within me, and have sorrow in my heart day after day? How long shall my enemy exalt himself over me? Consider, and answer me, O Lord my God; Lighten the eyes to behold your face in the pitch-like-darkness, lest I sleep of death".

Job also suffered great despair and depression, saying: "So that I would choose strangling and death rather than these my bones. I loathe my life; I would not live forever. Let me alone, for my days are a breath. (futility) Job 7: 15, 16) Job was a righteous man who was tested by God under overwhelming misfortune. In Chapter 10: I am weary of my life and loathe it! I will give free expression to my complaint; I will speak in the bitterness of my soul".

But Job persevered through the agonies and calamities. After God spoke to him, Job says: "I have rashly uttered what I did not understand, things too wonderful for me, which I did not know. I had heard of you by the hearing of the ear; but now my (spiritual) eye sees you. Therefore I loathe my words and abhor myself, and repent in dust and ashes."

The Lord blessed Job's later years more than the beginning. After this, Job lived a hundred and forty years. So Job died, an old man and full of days. (James 5: 11)

Apart from the Bible, suicide has touched people from all corners, and paths imaginable. From Socrates y too Brutus, and Cleopatra and Mark Antony, that I describe more about in Chapter Two.

In the pagan world of the Greeks and Romans, suicide was not strictly opposed, and were more lenient toward the act of suicide. It was, in fact, the Christians who condemned it in 452 at the counsel of Aries, as being the work of the Devil.

There was intense debate throughout the churches in the Middle Ages concerning suicide and martyrdom. It wasn't until the later part of the 17th century that Catholic doctrine was decided upon in the disputed areas of suicide.

Suicide, to the ancient Greek philosophers, like Aristotle, believed that it robbed the community services from one of its members. Plato sided with Aristotle, and extended this practical opinion to include that the human body belonged to God, therefore the destruction of Divine property and law. And although the Romans were pragmatic in their attitudes about the taking of ones life, they openly approved of a patriotic death by suicide. This distinction wasn't extended to Mark Antony, however, and they scorned his death. The Romans didn't disapprove of Antony because he killed himself, but that he killed himself for love.

Suicide as an event of social protest was used by a tribe in the south American rain forest. The Kaiowes tribe committed a mass suicide to bring international attention to their claim that their government was robbing them of their land. Buddhist monks of South Vietnam during the 1960's, protested against their president, Ngo Dinh Diem, by becoming human torches until they burned to death in the street.

A "History of Suicide" falls into a dark category of behavior in mankind. A conclusion to this chapter is a final word to the wise from Solomon: "THERE IS NO WORK OR DEVICE OR KNOWLEDGE OR WISDOM IN THE GRAVE WHERE YOU ARE GOING." (Ecclesiastes 9: 10)

Chapter Two

Grim Illusions Of The Depressed

The disturbed, unstable mind is under the illusion that their thinking is rational. Suicide can become an obsession under this particular illusion that life is no longer worth living.

Depressed people can be "masters of illusion." to quote psychiatrist and author, David Burns, M.D. Some illusory sleight-of-hand and our minds play tricks on us. Things can become distorted by looking at our lives in a negative way. Bipolar and depressives are especially susceptible to errors in thinking, even when successful and accomplished. Depression and negative thinking creates illusions and distortions of our perception of the world and our place in it.

Even in the least of matters where our thinking directs our decision making, there are influences at work in our brain. Just the mere awareness of that fact can affect outcome. For example, most of us have a "blind spot" That's the tendency not to counteract or compensate for one's personal prejudice. Another influence we may not be consciously aware of, called the "bandwagon effect." is a leaning toward a belief or opinion simply because a number of other people do. And "framing." is when the mind uses a too narrow approach, or limits their perspective of the situation or problem.

What we think, and how we go about our cognitive business also has an effect on our minds. Sometimes we aren't aware of our programming, and if made aware—our thinking patterns disrupted—it's possible that a tendency, or a negative belief system, can be turned around or reshaped. To continue, "hyperbolic discounting"—when the tendency is to have a stronger preference for more immediate payoffs, the closer to the present both payoffs are.

And—"irrational escalation" is the penchant for making irrational decisions based upon rational decisions in the past to justify present behavior. Another is the "mere exposure effect." an undue liking for things merely because there's a familiarity with them—or the other way around. (disliking things)

The next is "rebellion." the reactance urge, to do the opposite of what someone wants you to do out of a need to resist a perceived attempt to inhibit or restrain personal freedom or choices. A couple more that I thought would be of interest in ways our minds work: "Selected perception." is the tendency for expectations and wishful thinking to affect perception; and, "the illusion of control." which is a tendency to believe we can control or at least influence outcomes that realistically won't happen.

What we learn to perceive can translate into a hopeful purpose and positive values, or a continual exposure to negativity may propel one into depression and those outcomes. It is possible to break or disrupt negative tendencies and patterns, and to stay off the path that ends up in the illusion that life isn't worth living.

The greatest suicidal risks are bipolar and depressives. This is because depression is the greatest predictor of whether a person will attempt or complete suicide.

A high degree of stress over an extended period of time usually increases right before a suicide attempt. The stress can come from psychological as well as physiological reasons. Family genes play a part and also the family itself. Sometimes the members of the family not only are often a cause of the suicidal behavior but just as often excuse themselves as a resource.

Taking a close look at depression and breaking it down can give insight into suicidal thinking. Anyone who has suicidal thoughts is self-absorbed in their own self-made bubble they believe is invisible and also invincible.

It's important to find a way to get their attention outside of themselves. Bursting their bubble of the grim illusion that they are not valued or worthwhile is a good thing to do. The true reality of all our lives is that God deems us worth enough to have his son, Jesus Christ die on the cross for us, resurrected to give us a way to salvation and eternal life. Christ took our place, so God believes we have some redeeming value. A different reasoning and thinking can occur in a mind of faith.

Mental health professionals can help to organize and direct the irrational thinking of a depressed person. Intervening may be called for in the form of guidance and support, and even medication because they are under the illusion that nothing is wrong. The warning signs at the front of this book aren't looked upon as deadly to them.

Depression weakens a person's ability to function in a normal way. It affects a life in everyday matters, including the ability to work, eat or sleep. It keeps people from experiencing any joy or hope in their lives. The things that gave them pleasure and enjoyment before, don't anymore. A major depression is debilitating, and can deepen into despair and suicide attempts or completions.

A milder form of depression is called, dysthymia. The mood is so pervasive and persistent that it dominates the personality of the depressed person. It can seem that's "just the way they are."

The "highs and lows" of bipolar disorder—also known as manic depression—is a part of the equation in discussing grim illusions of the depressed. I characterized bipolar as a "radical psychological shift in moods," primarily mania and depression. Depression is a put-down to the system. Whether it's reactive or chemical, you feel defeated, hopeless, drained of emotion and interest in life. It's almost impossible to function, to make decisions, to feel worthwhile, and suicide is on your mind. You're not sleeping, or you're sleeping too much. You may be irritable and cry easily, and you're always tired. And then there's the unrelenting despair.

Clinical depression isn't about "pulling yourself up by your boot-straps," as the misguided wife's notion of it implies in Chapter Two's cartoon. It's a profound and disabling condition that impacts the mind, heart and soul. Whether it's chemical or self-deluding, the result is the same; negative, harmful symptoms that erode or cut-short a valuable life.

Research on depression has suggested that over twenty million Americans are suffering with some kind of depression. Also revealed is the fact that maybe a third of them actually go for help and treatment. Those that do, however, get a boost in mood where they can figure things out, hopefully and with faith.

Depression increases the risk of suicide. All the symptoms and states of mind and moods that it brings, also carry with it thoughts of ending one's life. The outcome of a seriously depressed person can be a suicide. Reports garnered in this area conclude that as many as 15 per-cent of those who are clinically depressed are deaths by suicide. It goes on to say that these attempts and completions are an act of extreme distress that requires some type of resolution and is wrong to think of it as a bid for attention. However, "leaving someone alone," isn't the answer. Isolation is merely the illusory, self-protective mechanism that can lead to a suicide.

From the NARSAD Journal, Fall of 1999, vol 11: "My greatest personal shock happened after I had been with NARSAD for four years when my oldest grandson took his life at Georgia Tech in his third year. When I went to the morgue in Atlanta, they handed me my grandson's bag, and in it was the address of a prominent psychiatrist whom he never visited or made an appointment with. He had told his mother, Kitty, he was having some depression and he felt like he needed help, but it pains me that she had not told me this. Kitty said that she did not want me to worry. Well, I want you to know that is denial and it is a sin that we are all guilty of. I assume that the more closely we are associated with people that need help in our families, the more we tend to deny it. Depression runs in our family. I have a nephew who, the year after he finished college, became manic depressive and attempted suicide. Luckily, he did not succeed."

When discussing the grim illusions of the suicidally depressed, the ethical aspect questions, "Is it moral?" I understood that those who commit suicide have an unstable mind, so it wouldn't be a rational act. Nor can we deny that life comes from God, and some accountability of what we do with it. The philosopher, Emanuel Kent, contended that suicide is the most serious of crimes because it is man's rejection of his mortality. For centuries the ending of ones life has been declared an unethical act, by both theologians and philosophers.

In the new world we live in today, that view is challenged. There are societies in the U.S., and in England that promote suicide as an ethical action and a "rational" choice, being an alternative to life. Their argument for siding with suicide is that it's all about "autonomy." They seek control over a destiny that they feel has too much suffering or loneliness. The obvious weakening of traditional values and moral decline has fostered those pro-suicide societies. A noted psychiatrist and sociologist, David Peretz, explains it this way: "Under the unprecedented stress of recent decades, denial mechanisms are breaking down, and we have become increasingly vulnerable to the threats of intensely painful feelings of anxiety, fear, panic, rage, guilt, shame, grief, longing, loneliness or degradation at the time of death. If people can't deal with their fear of death and dying, they seek new ways to adapt. They find comfort in the illusion, "It will not be done to me, I will do it myself." Peretz goes on to say that he believes that is a dangerous motivation because it encourages the harmful illusion of personal omnipotence.

A heralding to new extreme individualism of autonomous suicide becomes a detriment not only to ourselves, but to our family and community. These are times to help and to encourage and admit to one another and to God that we are in need and at times of suffering, inadequate and need help. Doing this, we engage in God's purpose in living, not succumbing by suicide. To adhere to an ultimate self-defeatism is not just a grim illusion, but a vain admission to, "I can do it all by myself."

The act of self-destruction by suicide as a solution to end suffering is a serious delusion and miscarriage of a God-given life. No matter what stage of life we're in from conception to the term limits of old age, we abort God's purpose and His will by committing suicide.

To think rationally about one's life would be to exclude the illusion of solving problems by suicide. But, anyone who is caught up in this illusion automatically becomes an accessory to the crime of self-murder.

Distorted thinking can be a problem in itself. Our belief system generates how we think and behave. Outside conditions, other's opinions of us, peer pressure and social expectations—to name a few—can influence us for a negative experience. Add to the mix our undeniable human nature, personal affinities, inclinations and experiences.

Negative thinking patterns in melancholy can become an obsessive addiction. If we understand that depression isn't just emotions out of control or even an imbalance of chemicals, but patterns and processes of how we habitually think, then change is possible.

If we believe, by training, experience or conditioning, any negative input under vulnerable conditions, our minds are fixated in an emotional dependency. It becomes blame and denial, until we learn to decide and to control our thinking process.

We can't tolerate the fantasy of acting as if the depressed person has an intrinsic knowing of how to stop being depressed. The temporary fix of escapism through alcohol, food and other satiations and distractions, only extend and deepen life's problems because they become, "the source," and thereby, the re-enforcer.

Transformation and change are possible, but foundation, and our ultimate frame of reference will determine the quality and direction of any long-term changes. We have to factor in genetic and environment and memories that will influence our habits, conscious and unconscious. We unknowingly rely on conditioned responses, herd instincts and personal hopes and fears. What is actually in our control and is a true perception of how we envision our life is complex.

An emotion that goes along with depression is the feeling of being smothered or trapped by someone or a circumstance. When the situation is perceived as unbearable, and change isn't forthcoming, despair can set in and suicide can become an option.

The grim illusion of the depressed is that there is no way out. It's an illusion that could be remedied if a path could be seen through the fog. Clear thinking isn't available to the depressed mind. Professional help at this juncture could be able to see what you aren't able to, and steps to take to avoid the trap.

When the path or solution to the crisis isn't discovered, the illusions will become even grimmer and more entrenched.

The illusion of curing ourselves by, "If only," we were this or that, and painful memories could be muted by alcohol, or other numbing activities to excuse abuses long not forgotten; all only serve to reinforce illusions of the depressed. To continue on with the insanity of illusion is to doom the self to an inconsolable position.

It's argued that we need both negative and positive emotions. Shelley Taylor, a health psychology professor at U.C.L.A., and Jonathan Brown, a psychology professor at Southern Methodist University, argue the opinion that positive illusions are all that are needed to maintain a sense of well being in life.

The psychologists' basis for this reasoning is that positive illusion and distortion of feedback that actually enhance the state of our mental outlook, while a truthful reckoning of our self-image and society may cause a feeling of not measuring up in the ways of the world. And if the psychologists are correct in the perception of truth, then a condition called depression will follow.

Another psychologist, Roy Baumeister's "optimal margin of illusion" hypothesis: "There is an optimal margin of illusion for healthy, psychological functioning—a small positive distortion is optimal. Those who distort less than the optimal level have too realistic a view which is depressing; this may cause them to be hesitant to take on more challenging projects that could lead to success." He goes on to say that some illusions—or distortion of reality—is called for to survive, for people who suffer with severe depression tend to be negative and pessimistic. Since this is also what can be called an extreme realism, it can become an illusion that is a threat to a sense of well-being which can lead to depression, despair and suicidal thoughts. It could be called a chain-reaction that had its beginnings with Adam and Eve who in turn passed it down in a chain-like bondage that links you and me to death. "By one man sin entered into the world, and death by sin; and so death passed upon all men, for that all have sinned". Romans 5:12. "In Adam all die." I Corinthians 15:22.

What is true is that most human beings live mostly in some degree of illusion in "unrealistically positive views of the self, exaggerated perceptions of personal control, and unrealistic optimism," said Jonathan Brown.

Summing it up, according to Brown and Taylor, these illusions of a positive nature can create a more positive outlook, and raised self-esteem. A more positive sense for their future is a genuine way to reverse a depressed state of mind, they conclude.

Being depressed "narrows the framing," (when the mind uses a too narrow approach, or limits their perspective of the situation or problem) causing relationships and everyday problems to distort, and a feeling of loss of control sets in, setting a person up for a cycle of negativity. And that becomes their make-up, their frame of reference on solving problems.

Once negative anchors have been set in the mind, the symbols are easily activated. The fear of tackling something new can translate to, "What's the use? It probably won't work anyway." What triggers someone is complex and individual, but recognizing exactly where "the light goes out," can lead to overcoming the next time it happens, and making more positive references.

When a friend, counselor or pastor assists in re-framing a difficult circumstance, and helps the one in trouble see a workable solution, it won't be effective unless "triggers" are dealt with. If you get a handle on drinking or drug use, for example, then choose to return to hang out with friends who still drink or use drugs—it's a set-back. Or, one trots right back to an abusive boyfriend or husband; or maybe it's a gambling casino, that exposure to whatever your poison is will most likely set in motion the suicidal urges all over again.

The reason that depressed people isolate themselves is to avoid the triggers. They feel vulnerable since they are already depressed and on the edge. The world, people, family or job, become symbols—reminders—"Did you get that degree yet;" "Are you married yet?" (not even looking) There's an old saying that goes," It does no good to lock the barn door after the horse gets out." That applies to "Trigger"—pun intended. In other words, we have to learn what they are and then learn methods to stop, control or reduce whatever is overwhelming, degrading, exhausting, and strangling the hope out of us.

Remember the children's story, *Goldy Locks And The Three Bears?* One bowl of porridge was too hot, the second bowl the bear set down in front of her, she tasted it and it was too cold. BUT, the next bowl of porridge was "just right." The moral of the story for a bipolar or unstable mind who has suicidal tendencies is this: Avoid extremes, because the momentum of "obligatory consequences" of the high to low, (like a rubber ball) will keep you bouncing all over the place. Shoot for a balance, a feeling of evenness.

It's a little like not allowing yourself to get "too hot under the collar," or "too cold," either. I believe that when we choose to develop patience, forgiveness and gratitude in our lives, we can deal with what's set before us. But, worrying and obsessing about tomorrow only drags you back to square one. Jesus said that, "Sufficient unto the day are the troubles therein." A bipolar tends to over-do, obsess and escalate. This extends to worrying, too, which is negativity and shows a lack of faith. Once I recognize this, I "lock-in," by reminding myself of that verse, and it immediately reigns in that nag, negativity. It's simple and it works because I believe it. Jesus also said, "I am the way, the truth, and the life . . ." John 14: 6. Faith cometh by hearing, and hearing by the word of God.

Oswald Chambers (*My Utmost For His Highest*) brings up the fact that, if we were not capable of being depressed, we wouldn't be alive. He said, "A human being is capable of depression, otherwise there would be no capacity for exultation. There are things that are calculated to depress, things that are of the nature of death; and in taking an estimate of yourself, always take into account the capacity for depression." He writes in the Daily Devotional that depression can turn us away from the ordinary, everyday things of God's creation. I think of a starry sky, a beautiful sunrise or a glorious sunset; holding a newborn child, the scent of rain, the special Fall air when football season is in the air, or the aroma of dinner cooking in the kitchen, a puppy in the arms of your child, Spring flowers after a harsh winter, kindness from a stranger, and angels we know are watching over us during serendipitous moments of God's love and grace. It brings to mind one of the songs from the award-winning movie, "The Sound Of Music,"—'My Favorite Things,' and Julie Andrews, as Maria, sang about 'cream colored ponies, crisp apple—strudel, and rain-drops on roses,' the lyrics enchant us to remember a few of our favorite things, 'when the dog bites, or the bee stings!' We all have favorite memories that depression makes us forget.

These are the ordinary, common things. To quote Oswald Chambers again, "God tells us to do the most natural, simple things—and as we do them we find that He is there. The inspiration which comes to us in this way is an initiative against depression". He goes on to write that if we do a thing in order to overcome depression, the depression will deepen. The drinking or other unhealthy methods to deaden the conscience are examples. Oswald Chambers then wrote, "If the Spirit of God makes us feel intuitively that we must do the thing, and we do it, the depression is gone . . ."

When grim illusions of the depressed enters into love and romantic relationships, irrational behavior can be deadly. One of the most famous examples is Romeo and Juliet, characters in a play by Shakespeare. It seems that the character, Romeo, was deeply despondent and melancholy with forlorn love for his Juliet. Cast down, Romeo walks around in Act One, "Wallowing in self-pity," passionately evokes, "Love is a smoke raised with the fume of sighs." Filled with grief that his love is not returned, he seems incapable of any rational thought that if he dies, then Juliet's love will never be his. The last lines, "Being in night, all this but a dream. Too flattering-sweet to be substantial." Sleep being th symbol for death, and "sweet," suggests their "dark fall" by grim illusions. The impetuousness and the flaw of pride led to the illusion of unrequited love.

Unrequited love runs through the theme of many of Shakespeare's plays where death occurs. Another romantic couple with the consequence of tragedy is Mark Antony and Cleopatra. Under the influence of strong emotion, the deceived Mark Antony says of Cleopatra: "This foul Egyptian hath betrayed me." He vows to kill her while Cleopatra regrets her treachery and schemes to recapture his love by having word sent to him that she has killed herself, dying with his name on her lips. Locked away in her own monument, she awaits the rescue of her love, Mark Antony. But, this didn't happen as she planned. Instead, he feels that since Cleopatra is "dead" that his life isn't worth living. He pleads with one of his aides to run him through with a sword, but Eros does not have the heart to do that, and kills himself. Then Mark Antony attempts to do it himself and die on the sword rather than go on living without Cleopatra. He only wounds himself instead. In a great deal of pain, word comes to him that Cleopatra is alive. In great distress, he is lifted, hoisted up to her in the monument, and there, dies in her arms. The ending, and the end of Cleopatra is that she was betrayed and taken into custody by the Romans. She kills herself by the poison of the asp.

This illusion of unrequited love and life is no longer worth living has been around since Shakespeare, and goes back to the Old Testament. Melancholy and creativity are also linked.

From *Radical Psychological Mood Shifts*, "God gave me some creative talent. Creativity and mood disorder, more succinctly put: insanity and creativity, have been connected for centuries. From poets, like myself, to politicians, and actors, melancholy and mania have been written and speculated about. Not all creative people have mood disorder, and not all mood disordered people are creative. In my case, I can relate.

Some of the names of the well-known manic depressives that come to mind are: Ernest Hemingway, Vincent Van Gogh, Sylvia Plath, Winston Churchill, Handel, Howard Hughes, and actress Patty Duke. Hemingway shot himself to death, Plath, a poet, also committed suicide, as did the writer, F. Scott Fitzgerald. We know at least that these creatives were emotionally disturbed.

But, grim illusions of the depressed and suicide are related. And illusions of romantic, unrequited love as "reason" to commit suicide. A man in Florida threatened to kill himself after his girlfriend broke-up with him. Daren Ramphad was a 25 year-old pilot for a skydiving enterprise, took off in a single-engine plane. His dead body was later found in the wreckage of the plane that he'd crashed into a nearby field.

A modern day romance is another illustration of illusory expectations. A mother of three small children and recently separated. At her divorce, there was an agreement on custody of the children. Months later, she met someone, on an internet chat room. She had just moved with her children into a four bedroom from a much smaller place. The guy, who was a student at a nearby community college, moved in with them. He was studying to become a graphic designer. Shortly, she became pregnant with his daughter. He graduated from college and got a job in San Francisco as a graphic designer. They bought a home.

He became unhappy at work, stayed out late at bars and avoided her. He found another job at a French owned software company that made video games. Not long after, he told her that he'd fallen in love with the woman who was his new boss.

At first, the couple tried counseling, but unsuccessfully. Hostile feelings erupted between them, and, according to him, she threatened to kill herself and left. Worried, he reported her disappearance to the Contra Costa's Sheriff 's Department. The next day the woman sent an e-mail to him that stated: "My body will not be found," and "this is my last e-mail."

Another category of the grim illusions of the depressed revolves around money. A prime example is the stock market crash of 1929 that gave momentum to the Great Depression. It's a matter of record that during the 20th century, a majority of the capital in the United States was represented by stocks. A corporation had capital and ownership of the corporation in turn took the form of shares of stock. The Stock Exchange on Wall Street in New York was the most important. There was an unprecedented, long boom in the 1920's. Stocks more than quadrupled in value between 1920-1929. A lot of investors believed that stocks were a sure bet, and borrowed heavily to invest more money in the market.

But, the bubble burst. In 1929 the Stock Exchange dropped and plunged, and in 1932 and '33 it hit bottom. Down at about 80 per cent and profoundly effected the economy. The demand for goods fell, and mainly it was because people felt poor, because of the losses in the stock market. And fresh investments could not be financed through the sale of stock, because people wouldn't buy stock.

The biggest effect was chaos in the banking system as banks tried to collect on loans made to stock market investors whose holdings had little or no value. At that time in history, the banking system virtually ceased to operate.

Caught unawares, firms tightened their belts, and reduced their purchase of goods, production in turn cut back. Consumers held back too, afraid of losing a paycheck, falls in prices and deflation ended up as the Great Depression. Milton Friedman said that the Depression was, "a consequence of an incredible sequence of blunders in monetary policy. "But those in control of that policy during the early 1930's, believed that they were only adhering to the same gold-standard principles as their predecessors." Complex and difficult to explain the reasons why, it was the only "Great Depression."

The great depression that followed because of lost fortunes, wages and opportunities, mismanagement and fear, led to many taking their own lives; some jumping to their deaths. They irrationally placed more value on the paper money they inordinately put too much stock in—than their own life.

A big issue in our culture is euthanasia. This "grand illusion" is also called by its right name—" physician, or other, assisted suicide." Basically, it's a self-induced death whereby drugs or other means are provided by the one who assists the suicide.

Euthanasia and assisted suicide advocates gives the argument that, "It's for their own good;" "It's an act of compassion," hence the term, "mercy killing." These types are essentially saying, "You're better off dead." Compassion means kindness and assisting in alleviating pain and suffering, not, I believe, eliminating the one suffering.

With today's medical technology, it is possible to relieve pain substantially for patients who are terminally ill. There is pain management for all circumstances, and information to the public assures of breakthroughs that ensure that a patient can be made comfortable.

The strident advocates who proclaim, "the right to die," may actually carry the meaning—an "obligation to die."

Chapter Three

Abuse Is Deadly: The Ways Of Suicide

In the dictionary "*abuse*" is defined by my American Heritage dictionary of The English Language, Third Edition as: v. 1) abused, abusing. 2.) To use wrongly or improperly. 3.) To hurt or injure by maltreatment. 4.) To insult; revile. n. 1.) Misuse; drug use. 2.) Physical maltreatment, 3) Insulting or course language.

The degradation and insult of abuse can fall under many categories: mental and emotional, verbal abuse, cold indifference or abandonment—anyone who has been abused knows that vileness has touched their lives. If the event(s) happened to a child up to the age of eighteen, then pure rage is the emotion one feels toward these people they needed to love and protect them, and primarily the people they needed to love.

What generally happens is that the child is left alone to resolve it the best way they are able to. That translates to believing that there's something deeply wrong with them because those in the family circle abuse them further by cold indifference and blame, instead of where it rightly belongs—to the abuser. The one that is harmed and maligned begins to pretend that it didn't happen, and the rage becomes buried under feelings of sadness and illusion.

However, it isn't really forgotten. They create another identity for themselves. Someone else. Maybe it's their sexual identity, or how they identify themselves at a basic level of identification, or a standard that separates for a sense of belonging and safety on many levels. It can become illusions and fantasies that keep on mirroring the lost image, and for the life of them can't imagine what they're supposed to be about. If we follow the "yellow brick road," we might discover that as adults, we're likely to suffer with depression, addictions and abusive relationships.

In my research and study of abuse, sexual abuse basically magnifies feelings of worthlessness in a minor child. For the abuser it isn't all about sex. He may even be married. The molester wants to demean, degrade and control. Having to live in this kind of treatment and environment causes a disconnect in this young person. Emotional and psychological problems of all kinds will begin to manifest, and becomes a continual nightmare. As an adult, if the nightmare illusion isn't dispelled, then for the one encapsulated the only way to "break free"—to their irrational thinking—is to commit suicide.

Sexual abuse and suicide was studied at a Crisis Intervention Program of a community health center in California. The results of that study confirms that sexual abuse victims were at greater risk to commit suicide, and more likely to reveal suicidal thoughts when interviewed. Further investigation reports that sexual abuse was directly linked with suicide attempts of abuses which happened in childhood and adolescence. All of the women interviewed who experienced sexual abuse in their youth, had as a result, psychological damage and dysfunction which increases depression and suicidal thoughts.

Of the different ways of suicide, which includes depression, drug and alcohol abuse, sexual, and domestic abuse, major illness whether mental or physical—all of which can play a part in suicide attempts, sexual abuse is the one most associated with attempts to commit suicide.

There is evidence from my study on sexual abuse and suicide that suggests that people who were sexually molested are more likely to think about ending their lives. A new report says the risk is even higher if the assault occurred in childhood.

"Sexual assault is associated with an increased lifetime rate of attempted suicide," a quote from Dr. Jonathan Davidson, of Duke University Medical Center in Durham, N. Carolina. The recent study of as many as 3,000 people in N. Carolina, 67 reported having been sexually assaulted. Of these, about 15 per-cent had attempted suicide, as compared to less than 2 per-cent of the people who did not have that history of a sexual assault. This was reported in the January '08 issue of the Archives of General Psychiatry. Dr. Davidson concluded with, "The immensely damaging effect of such an event can not be stressed too strongly, particularly in individuals with other vulnerability factors, such as family dysfunction, genetic or familial vulnerability to (psychological problems) and other developmental problems."

Further information taken from Psychiatric News (listed in References) is that people who were victims of childhood sexual assault may exhibit strong tendencies to create ways to escape and to stop the emotional pain well into middle life and even older adulthood.

That time heals all wounds doesn't ring true when it concerns being abused in childhood. "Many times with older hospitalized adults, they may minimize th impact of early life experiences," said Nancy Talbot, PhD. In a study, Talbot and colleagues evaluated 127 women over the age of fifty who were admitted to a psychiatric unit who had been diagnosed with major depression. In that group of women, 18 of them reported sexual abuse at an early age, described as, "unwanted sexual contact before age 18."

Of those 18, fifteen (83%) had attempted suicide, and 12 (67%) had been hospitalized multiple times.

The Centers for Disease Control and Prevention report that suicide is uncommon among children the rate of suicide attempts, and deaths by suicide increases dramatically during the teen years. Suicide is the third-leading cause of death for 15-24 year-olds, according to the Center.

When an adolescent is surrounded by a good supportive system of family, friends, church, and activities, then they have a better than average chance to develop in a natural, healthy manner, and thereby learn how to cope and deal with the realities of life. However, it's definitely not a perfect world, and a child or teen can be abused by merely turning on the television, or going on the internet, or videos, music, and the wide world of Hollywood and movies. More teens in this day who are victims of sexual assault are in a higher-risk category for suicide.

All kinds of child abuse exists. And no matter what the abuse—it always has a devastating effect on the child. I believe the most insidious of all, is mental and emotional abuse. The assault of a child's spirit and mind is far worse.

The definition of emotional abuse is any behavior that interferes with a child's mental health, or social development. This would include belittling, name-calling, demeaning negativity, shaming and cursing the child. Emotional/mental abuse is also withholding affection, acceptance, and even discipline that would nurture and instill a sense of belonging and well-being. Causing a child to feel invisible in any or all of these areas is abuse more reprehensible than being beaten within an inch of your life. Physical wounds heal. A child needs to be hugged, told they are loved, supported and not criticized, or worse—ignored when there is hurt, or even achievement. Invisible. What kind of people, you might wonder, could be so destructive.

For that person, it becomes an ongoing struggle to live in surroundings that becomes a world where no one can be trusted, and safety turns into detachment, and coping behavior takes an extreme form of unhealthy risks. This self-destructive behavior could last for years to come, and have such a damaging effect, that drugs and alcohol abuse is tried—and becomes an addiction. A suicide is tried—only once. That's the real danger of emotional, mental or sexual abuse.

When there's emotional/mental abuse in an adult relationship, it is a pattern of behavior used against another person to break their will. They want to bring that person under their control.

Controlling behavior can be identified by intimidating tactics to pressure a person into submission and make them comply. Dominance and control is their aim.

Some objectives of a *verbal abuser* in order to control their victim:

1. Diminish your partner
2. Objectify your mate—make them a "thing."
3. Threaten and bully partner or person

It's amazing that some people may believe it's their right to dominate and have control over people. Domestic violence and divorce rates are escalating in America; although most who suffer are isolated and believe they're the only ones.

This makes it difficult to access and help end the oppression. It's made more difficult because usually the one in pain is told it's their fault. In a verbally abusive relationship it's about control. It's worse than physical abuse because of the subtle undermining strategies involved to gain control of someone. If you're in a relationship where you're being put-down and belittled, and you're tolerating it—dominance and control has been achieved by your abuser. The belittling techniques are calculated and deliberate. The continual "drip, drip, drip" into your mind and emotions are raw, is a brain-washing technique. Soon, you begin to believe the negative insults, you start doubting yourself, and the dangerous part is—you may start to think that your abuser is right. That's a slippery slope you don't want on. As he or she shoves and pushes and bullies you down into extreme doubt and self-blame, the name-calling begins. To solidify his position of control, the abuser will use humiliation. For example, he or she may enjoy calling you "crazy"—especially in front of other people. A bully wants to mainly intimidate and demean and demoralize their victim and remove self-esteem. The varying strategies, however, always involves isolating the victim. Examples: The rules are, he has to know where you're going and how long you'll be gone; he needs to know who all of your friends are, has control over what you wear. And they use guilt on your part, to make you do what he wants. Some use neglect, or the silent treatment—all done for dominance.

Manipulation and intimidation are sure signs of an abuser. He will deny, deny, and blame you, then refuse to discuss and resolve. Their aim is to keep you in emotional chaos—you're easier to manipulate and control in that state of mind.

Mental/emotional abuse is deadly. It's a virtual homicide on your soul—the cross-hairs are on their target—YOU! Their goal is to break your spirit That accomplished by your abuser—depression comes next. What can follow, and often does, is domestic violence and even suicide. Abuse is deadly in ways you might not even think of or imagine. Mostly it's psychological, in a relationship of one kind or another, but it can be cultural, political, social or "neighborly." Beware and be wary. These emotional/mental abusers are out to control even your beliefs, and your thoughts—will lie, steal, cheat and demoralize you to control every aspect of your life.

A form of abuse you may not be aware of is, "abuse by proxy." This means they use another person, a substitute, to do their dirty work. It could also be something legal, in writing, but authorized, that intends to harm. If you've been "hit below the belt," but it was delivered by "proxy," you were hit not only by the abuser, but his accomplice who shares the same motivation.

There's a strong link between domestic violence and suicide. Many more women die by suicide than suicide. To further investigate, researchers went through death certificates for each suicide in 2003 and cross-referenced them with court records to determine which had recorded cases involving domestic violence.

Barbara Hope, the executive director of East Lake Violence said, "Women get desperate and don't see any other alternative. It's something that we've known for a long time does happen. But we're not spending enough time discussing or talking about it."

The numbers grow each year, with teens being added as clients. The number is high with attempted suicides. One out of four women who were victims of domestic violence attempt suicide.

These are violent crimes against women—usually wives or girlfriends. The abuse isn't just physical beatings, but psychological attacks, also. As the research has stated, the attacks are meant to rob her of self-esteem and confidence, and turn the abuse into self-blame.

It's common for those women who are victimized to try and "change themselves to accommodate the perpetrator." Because the abuser has deliberately put them in emotional and mental chaos, their pain and confusion keeps them from seeing that they aren't to blame, and since this type of person refuses his conscience, it's very doubtful there's anything she can do to prevent the violence against her.

In cases of domestic violence, women often isolate themselves from family and friends and become severely depressed. A symptom of depression is feeling trapped with no workable solution to their situation. Suicide thoughts surface when counseling and supportive plans aren't made available or sought. This is a particular difficulty for women who live in rural areas.

Tragically, many children who live in homes with domestic violence, take their own lives. Children are deeply impacted by physical and emotional abuse. In general, the violence is done to the woman, and in a family setting—it's their parent, the mother. The abuser is either the biological father, step-parent, or live-in boyfriend. The children are horrified and feel helpless to stop it. They may become so distraught as to escape the pain by suicide.

The mother and children need to know that the best escape is to leave the abuser.

Domestic violence is reportedly one in three women are victimized sometime in their life. One in five who sustains physical injuries, goes to a hospital or doctor for any medical treatment. Maybe half of the incidents are reported to the police. Evidence has it that domestic violence doesn't stop—even though the abuser says he will—it only escalates. All women who stay with their attacker believing he will change, are at risk of becoming a murder victim at the hands of the same abuser.

Research of this subject of domestic violence gave evidence of the number of victims: annually in the U.S. Approximately 1,000, and as many as 1,600 women die at the hands of a spouse or male partner. The murder is a culmination of an extended period of battering. The number of domestic violence fatalities do not include the deaths by suicide of the women.

Other facts: the 11th leading cause of death in the United States is suicide, and the third leading cause for 15-25 year-olds. Homicide ranks somewhat lower. Statistics show that on average, someone kills themselves every eighteen minutes. Domestic violence is on the increase in our country.

Coroner's reports revealed that deaths in women due to assault were more likely to be the result of abuse in the home. To conclude: 90 per-cent of all domestic violence deaths happen to women.

Another category of deadly abuse involves substance abuse: drugs and alcohol. Data written about drug abuse and suicide indicate that in the

400,000 teen suicide attempts each year, over 5,000 between the ages of 15 and 24 will end in death.

In March of '08, four teen-agers, two sisters and their boyfriends were discovered inside a New Jersey garage, dead from exhaust fumes from the car's engine running in the closed garage. All four of the teens reportedly came from families of domestic violence and divorce.

Another thing they had in common was their use of drugs, and heavy drinking. The young men had been in a substance-abuse program. A close friend of theirs had fallen to his death from a cliff after hours of drinking. Although reported as an accident, the four friends, none could say he hadn't meant to do it. (fall)

The following day, two teen-age girls, 17 and 19, were also found dead inside a running car in Illinois. Friends of the girls said that one was despondent over her divorce and her two miscarriages. Both later unemployed, the two friends began drinking whiskey during the day and gradually lost touch with reality.

Under the influence of alcohol or drugs, people are more likely to commit suicide. The relationship between the already depressed and the depressant potential of alcohol and drugs can be lethal.

This connection is being explored by a trio of San Diego doctors. Their suicide study shows that above 60 per-cent of 133 suicide deaths investigated had a main psychiatric diagnosis of drug and alcohol abuse. And multiple substance abuse was common, naming cocaine, alcohol and marijuana the most used. The doctors, Richard C. Fowler, Charles L. Rich, and Deborah Young, agreed, "In addiction, our results indicate that the typical drug and alcohol abuse disorder was not subtle. It was usually characterized by multiple drug use for many years."

It's evident that drugs—mostly cocaine—used by young people can trigger severe depression that may create suicidal urges. Alcoholics experience the same kind of thing. Especially following a drinking binge, depression sets in and suicide is on their mind. Probably a number of suicides are wrongly reported or "covered up," or "run over," when actually they ran out onto a freeway while "under the influence."

There are people who have been warned by their doctors to "stop drinking" or it will eventually kill you. Even as alcoholics who develop liver disease, they openly admit and agree it will kill them, but go ahead and drink anyway. I think we can agree that this is a slow form of suicide.

The ways of suicide are many, and abuse in any form can be deadly. We all are familiar with the phrase, "children can be so cruel at that age."

Maybe it's a part of growing up, that cruel streak that's a thorn-in-the-side of our childhood.

School days aren't what they used to be. The educational system of today is an abuse in itself. Most parents are sending their children off to school naïve and unschooled with what is being taught—indoctrinated is closer to the truth. And, of course, what they are not being taught.

The school children of this period of time, have cell phones with cameras, and ways to send and receive messages by texting one another. And children can be cruel in more modern ways: there's blogging used to taunt and demean. "Mean" is their cruel intent. Selected victims are harassed and verbally stalked on-line to the point of psychological trauma and vulnerable to suicide.

In my research on "abuse can be deadly" and its connection to suicide, I wanted to include the real, emotional, physical, and even sexual abuse—by children, that is "bullying." What is a bully? The "controller" discussed in the segment about domestic violence—is a bully. A bully will walk all over your rights, use any tactic to gain control of the situation or a person. When push comes to shove—it's the one pickin' on the little guy, or intimidating or threatening someone who is vulnerable or weaker. It's always intentional, and not just "now and then," but a part of their personality and character.

"Bullying can seriously affect children's mental health, self-esteem, thoughts about suicide, health and academic work," states Susan Limber, PhD, a professor at Clemson University's Institute On Family and Neighborhood Life, in Clemson, South Carolina. In explaining the In explaining the bully behavior, Dr. Limber says that no matter what their background, a bully acts in a particular way. They push around the weaker kids, the ones who back off from confrontation. A bully is anti-social as a rule. A Dr. Espelage adds, "They may be involved in dating or marital violence or workplace harassment," because usually they continue their anti-social behavior beyond schoolyard bullying, and into the rest of their lives.

The bully abuse that turns deadly is now a term—it's "bullycide"—defined as a suicide caused by bullying and depression. It's become a part of our culture and our language. From the book, *Bullied To Death*, the author, Jo Lynn Carney, points out that, "victims of chronic peer abuse run an increased risk of suicide." She further argues that many students are exposed to risk of bullying and violence in their schools and communities and at home. She stated that, "Over a quarter of a million students per month are being physically attacked in the course of a school day. Carney concluded, "For some young people those external threats create a hopelessness and depression that can lead to suicidal thoughts or actions."

This is the story of two young boys, Mitchell Johnson, 13, and Andrew Golden, 11. According to classmates—these two were bullies. Their quest for control grew to an out of control violent ambush on students and teachers.

It happened in March of '98. Police reported that the two boys ambushed the students and teachers outside West Side Middle School in Jonesboro, Arkansas. Armed with three stolen rifles and four handguns, they deliberately evacuated the classrooms by setting off the fire alarm, then opened fire on kids and teachers as they came out. Four students and a teacher were murdered that day, and 11 others were wounded.

Even with the outbreak of school shootings, bullying and violence in the school is largely ignored. The National Center for Education Statistics National Household Education Survey, 1993, reported that most students in grades 6 through 12, about 16 per-cent were victims of bullying in the past school year.

The problem is overlooked and hidden, not talked about openly by victims or witnesses who are often threatened. By either pretending that bullying and violence "don't exist in our school district," to turn the other way while children are being abused, bullied, molested, and murdered while in their charge is a gross, malevolent symptom of tyranny.

School bullying isn't restricted to the school yard or the classroom. The school bully is now in cyberspace: Siannil Roughley was at the home of a friend one day. She came across a website that appeared like any teen-age girl's homepage. It was designed with a pink background covered with hearts and glitter. Siannil, 13, scrolled down, and stopped, horrified at what she saw. A photo of herself and the caption—"Well, dis iz da slag Siannil athat no one loikes coz she's a dity geebo. Piz sign da shout box of st u think of her xx. She's a SLAG xx"

There were dozens of messages beneath. One of those messages told her to "f*** off die," and others said, "We're going to get you at school tomorrow." This page was hit more than 2,000 times.

When interviewed, 13 year old Siannil said she was terrified to go to school. "It was awful," she said, and added, "I wasn't sleeping, I began to think that maybe they were right, maybe I should just kill myself."

These come from the social networking sites that for the most part are harmless, but what can't be ignored is the malicious spreading of "cyberbullying" that is getting out of control.

Another 13 year-old, Stephanie Godwin, from Gloucester, was victimized by cyberbullying for a year. A continual flow of abuse came onto her website. Stephanie became so afraid that she stayed away from school. One of the messages said: "Gay! Ur a f****** fat cow and a fat f*** u wanna shut ur f****** mouth cos you is gonna get banged"

Bullies are bullies are bullies—even in cyberspace. And a bully, like a dog—can sense your fear, and that just emboldens them, the animal that they are. There are ways to counteract a feeling of helplessness and fear. There are techniques to neutralize a bully's attacks. In Chapter Ten and listed on the Resources page, you'll find useful resources. But, bullies of any stripe will usually walk on by if you, "stand tall and stand up for yourself in a courageous, but non-aggressive presence."

Maybe you have never thought of this next category of deadly abuse. No one has ever been brainwashed that realized, or were aware that it had taken place.

Since I believe that brainwashing ranks high on a list of deadly abuses, this next segment can help prepare you and prevent a bigger bully which is—tyrants who want to control your mind. By definition, brainwashing is:

Brainwashing—n. Intensive, forcible indoctrination aimed at replacing a person's basic convictions with an alternative set of fixed beliefs.

This research has discovered an open permission to share this information on brainwashing by Dick Sutphen's, The Battle For Your Mind.

Mr. Sutphen begins with: *The Three Brain Phases:*

The formulation for brainwashing began with Pavlov, the Russian scientist. In the early 1900's his work with animals opened the door to further investigation with humans. After the revolution in Russia, Lenin was quick to see the potential of applying Pavlov's research to his own ends.

Three distinct and progressive states of transmarginal inhibition were identified by Pavlov. The *first* is the *equivalent phase*, in which the brain gives the same response to both strong and weak stimuli. The *second* is the *paradoxial phase*, in which the brain responds more actively to weak stimuli than to strong. And the *third* is the *ultra-paradoxial* phase, in which conditioned responses and behavior patterns turn from positive to negative, or from negative to positive.

With the progressions through each phase, the degree of brainwashing becomes more effective and complete.

The usual first step in brainwashing or control of your mind, is to work on the *emotions* of an individual or group until they reach an abnormal level of anger, fear, excitement or nervous tension.

The progressive result of this mental condition is to impair judgment and increase suggestibility. The more this condition can be sustained or intensified, the more it compounds.

Once *catharsis* or the first brain phase has been reached, the complete mental takeover becomes easier. Existing mental programming can be replaced with new patterns of thinking and behavior.

Other often-used physiological weapons to modify normal brain functions are physical discomforts, regulation of breathing, (mantra chanting in meditation) the disclosure of awesome mysteries, special lighting and sound effects, intoxicating drugs.

The same results can be obtained by contemporary psychiatric treatment by electric shock treatments and even by purposely lowering a patient's blood sugar level with insulin injection.

Music is very suggestible. A beat of repetitive music usually close to a heart beat ranging from 45 to 75 beats per minute. It's very hypnotic and can generate an eyes-open altered state of consciousness in a high percentage of people. And, once you're in an alpha state, you are at least 25 times a more likely state to be suggestible as you would be in a full beta consciousness. Subconsciously, the beat of the music is recalled almost automatically and you respond according to the post-hypnotic programming.

You can watch for external signs of brainwashing. One will exhibit trance-like signs—body relaxation and slightly dilated eyes. A voice roll technique is employed when inducing a trance. It is a patterned, paced style used by hypnotists (although not considered brainwashing) and the technique is used by many lawyers. A voice roll can sound as if the speaker were talking to the beat of a metronome, a patterned style.

THE MENTAL ABUSE OF BRAINWASHING TECHNIQUES *TO PROTECT YOURSELF AGAINST:*

Cults and organizations and institutions in order to manipulate need to create a brain phase. And often, they need to do it in short order. Maybe a day or a week-end. The meeting or training takes place in an area where participants are cut off from the outside world: a private home, a remote or rural setting, or even a hotel ballroom.

Intimidation and agreements to do as the cult or organization wants—or they're asked to leave. They intentionally try to create anxiety and tension that hopefully causes even a slight malfunction of the nervous system, which in turn increases the brainwashing potential.

Next, look for them to present a schedule to be maintained that causes mental and physical fatigue. This is primarily accomplished by long hours in which the participants are given no opportunity for relaxation or reflection.

And the next technique is to increase the tension in the room or environment,

After that phase, the brainwashing goes to the next step: Uncertainty. There are many techniques to increase tension and generate uncertainty. Basically, the participants are concerned about being "put on the spot," or encountered by the trainers, guilt feelings are played upon, participants are tempted to verbally relate their innermost secrets to the other participants or forced to take part in activities that emphasize removing their masks. A very high profile, human-potential seminar, forces the participants to stand on a stage in front of the entire audience while being verbally attacked by the trainers. A public opinion poll, conducted a few years ago, showed that the number one most fearful situation an individual could encounter is to speak to an audience. It ranked above window washing outside the 85th floor of an office building. So, you can imagine the fear and tension this generates. Many faint, but most cope with the stress mentally until it goes away. They literally go into an alpha state which automatically makes them many times as suggestible as they normally are.

And another loop of the downward spiral of brainwashing is successfully effected.

The Fifth Phase is the introduction to jargon—new terms that have meaning only to the "insiders" who have participated in the training. Vicious language is also frequently used to purposely make participants uncomfortable.

Next to know about in order to not be manipulated is a tactic that withholds any humor until the participants sign on the dotted line or whatever their goal of agreement is for you. Then—merry-making and humor are highly desirable as a symbol of the new joy the participants now have.

Not to say that good doesn't result from participation in such gatherings. But, it is important for people to know what has happened, and be aware that continual involvement may not be to their best interest.

Cult gatherings or human-potential trainings are an ideal environment to observe first hand what is technically called "the Stockholm Syndrome."

This is a situation in which those who are intimidated, controlled or made to suffer, begin to love, and possibly admire their captors or controllers.

A word of warning from the resource, Dick Stutphen, "If you think you can attend such gatherings and not be affected, you are probably wrong." An example he gives if the case of a woman who went to Haiti on a Guggenheim Fellowship to study Haitian Voodoo. In her report she related how the music eventually induced uncontrollable bodily movement and an altered state of consciousness. Although she understood the process and thought herself above it, when she began to feel herself become vulnerable to the music, she attempted to fight it and turned away. Anger or resistance almost always assures brainwashing. A few moments later she was possessed by the music and began dancing in a trance around the voodoo house A brain phase had been induced by the music and excitement.

So, if you attend any such gatherings similar or dissimilar, in order to avoid the brainwashing abuse by not allowing or being affected, by staying detached, bringing no positive or negative emotion to surface. Few people can do this, however.

Once the initial "submission" (to whatever aim) cults and similar groups cannot have cynicism among the members. Members must respond to commands and do as they are told, otherwise they are dangerous to the organizational control. This is normally accomplished as a *three-step Decognition Process:*

Step One is Alertness Reduction: The controllers cause the nervous system to malfunction, making it difficult to distinguish between fantasy and reality. This can be accomplished in several ways. Poor diet is one. Sugared treats and refreshments throw your nervous system off. The more subtle of diets in some cults is the "only vegetable and fruit" diet, without the needed grains, nuts, seeds, dairy products, fish or meat. An individual on that diet becomes mentally spacey. Inadequate sleep is another primary way to reduce alertness, especially when combined with long hours of work or intense physical activity. Being bombarded with intense and unique experiences achieves the same result.

Step Two is Programmed Confusion:

You are mentally assaulted while your alertness is being reduced as in Step One. This is accomplished with a deluge of new information, lectures, discussions, groups, encounters or one-to-one processing, which usually amounts to the controller bombarding the individual with questions. During this phase of decognition reality and illusion often merge and perverted logic is likely to be accepted.

Step Three is Thought Stopping:

Techniques are used to cause the mind to go "flat." There are altered-state-of-consciousness techniques that usually initially induce calmness by giving the mind something simple to deal with and focusing awareness. The continuous use brings on a feeling of elevation and eventually hallucination. The result is the reduction of thoughts and eventually, if used long enough, the cessation of all thought and withdrawal from everyone and everything except that which the controller directs. The takeover is complete. It is important to be aware that when members or participants are instructed to use "thought stopping" techniques, they are told that they will benefit by so doing, be better at whatever, or find enlightenment.

There are three primary techniques for thought-stopping:

1. *Marching*—the thump, thump, thump beat literally generates self-hypnosis, and thus great susceptibility to suggestion.
2. *Meditation*—If you spend an hour to an hour and a half a day in meditation, after a few weeks there is a great probability that you will not return to full beta consciousness. You will remain in a fixed state of alpha for as long as you continue to meditate. This isn't bad if you do it yourself. But it is a fact you're causing your mind to go flat. Meditators on an E.E.G machine show conclusively that the more you meditate the flatter your mind becomes.
3. *Chanting*—and often chanting is meditation. All three techniques produce an altered state of consciousness. This may be good if YOU are controlling the process, for you also control the input. It's how much you want to be "out there" and suggestible. (conclusion of this segment)

The last segment of the chapter is about deadly abuse that Orwell might have written. Only it was written in the Post Independent, Colorado, and carried by w n b . (World Net Daily)

This is about a "home invasion" characterized by Jan Shiflett as a "nazi" (def: a member of the fascist political party that held power, 1933—'45, in Germany under Adolf Hitler) home invasion by a S.W.A.T. Team. According to the report, Jan Shiflett's son, 11 year-old Jon, was abducted by S.W.A.T. Team members and taken to a hospital after he was bruised "horsing around." The irate mother began warning members of her community of the "Nazi tactics" her family went through, and included a statement from the S.W.A.T.

That her "rights" were only "in the movies." The case involves Jon Shiflett, who sustained a bruise trying to grab the car door-handle on the car his sister was driving. Instead, he fell, hitting his head on the pavement. His parents treated the injury, rejecting the paramedics demands that they be allowed to take him to the hospital.

It was a day and a half later that S.W.A.T. Team members invaded their home in W. Colorado, near New Castle. They took Jon by force to a hospital where the doctor instructed that ice should be kept on his bruise, exactly the treatment his family had already provided.

Tina Shiflett, Jon's mother, wrote a letter to the editor of their local paper, "To awaken, to alert, and appall any who read it and hear the bells ringing."

"A fully armed S.W.A.T. Team broke into our home, slammed my children to the floor face down with their hands behind their backs and shoved a gun in my daughter's face and handcuffed her . . ." her letter said.

There was another letter to World Net Daily. In it she said: "An officer (SWAT) grabbed my daughter Beth (18 y/o) who also had a gun to her face, slammed her down and kneed her in the back and held her in that position . . . My sons Adam (14) and Noah (only 7) lay down willingly, yet they were still forced to put their hands behind their backs and were yelled at to keep their heads down.

"My daughter, Jeanette, was coming out from the back bedroom when she was grabbed, drug down the hallway, across a couch and slammed to the ground," she said. "The officer then began throwing scissors and screwdrivers across the room (out of reach, I suppose) and going through our cupboards.

"I asked if I could make a phone call and was told, "no." My daughter asked if that wasn't one of our rights. The reply was made, "That's only in the movies."

An unidentified person, possibly a paramedic, who had been told "no" to take Jon to the hospital, who gave information to a magistrate to issue a court order that Jon be taken into state custody and examined by a doctor.

Reportedly he was taken by S.W.A.T. Team members dispatched by the sheriff to the Shiflett's home at 11:00 p.m. at night, and they punched a hole in their front door, held guns on the other children in order to take Jon.

"The armed men in black masks took my son against his wishes to Grand River Hospital where he was examined by a doctor and interrogated by Social Services. No evidence was found that he had not been properly taken care of.

"To the S.W.A.T. Team members . . . . how far will you go in 'just doing your job' ? If you feel no guilt busting into an innocent family's home traumatizing young children and stomping the security found therein, will you follow more horrific orders?" she wrote.

"May I remind you that in Nazi Germany, outrageous, monstrous crimes were committed by soldiers 'just doing their job.' What will be next? Where will this stop?" she concluded.

The county sheriff, Lou Vallario was reported to have told Worl Net Daily: "I was given a court order by the magistrate to seize the child, and arrange for medical evaluation, and that's what we did," he said.

A neighbor had called paramedics, although Jon had been treated by his parents in a satisfactory manner. When the paramedics arrived, Tom Shiflett allowed them to see his son; since he had already taken care of the injury, refused their demands that he be seen by a doctor at a hospital.

The paramedics then talked to the city police, the sheriff's office, social workers and eventually the magistrate in order to get their way.

A court clerk in Garffield County, reportedly said that it was a juvenile matter and he could not comment on any aspect of the case, and he declined to leave a message for the magistrate, Lain Leoniak, who signed the court order.

There was, however, a forum that commented, gathering at the Rocky Mountain News which also carried news reports of the incident, took sides with Tina Shiflett, and wrote: "It's Just Me, 'Welcome to the coming socialist police state.' Said, "mr. Nice Guy, 'Police man shoots man in heart at a distant range, is not charged. Police cover up the events that proceed the death of someone in their custody; no one is charged. Police enter wrong apartment and shoot an unarmed man thinking a can is a weapon; no charges filed. But a kid bumps his head and his parents deem him to be o.k., the police knock the door in and start cuffing people.'"

One participant of the forum at the Denver Post responded in this manner: "Whoever it was that gave the order to do this should be thrown in jail. Illegal assaults on our privacy is why we need the second amendment. I don't see the police being this aggressive against illegal aliens, but they approach their work with this level of zest against citizens?? Heads should roll for this."

Abuse can be deadly. Abuse takes on many forms, as you have read, whether inflicted on us by outside forces, or we damage our own mind, body and spirit.

Answers won't come from political systems, mental and physical health professionals, or leaders at any level. Although knowledge is useful and essential, we have to respect our innate person hood and soul, given by God, working together from self-awareness and discernment.

It goes back to pride and ego, just look around you! Depravity being blatantly marketed—the indocrination of the masses. We play into their hands by surrendering the sovereignty of our souls. A victim mentality, like sheep, offering up one's throat—is a form of suicide.

Chapter Four

Unlikely Candidates Dark Fall—
Soldiers And Suicide

Suicide strikes on every front, and soldiers included in the ranks range from the lowest enlisted private, to bonafide colonels and well-known heroic WW II fliers. It seems to be an unlikely act because of how we perceive what a soldier personifies, but in fact, suicide was not uncommon in warfare and battles, revolutionary times or crusades all throughout history.

Historically, soldiers have committed suicide for such reasons as, to keep from becoming a prisoner of war, or being captured in some wars, to avoid slavery. This includes soldiers of other countries. At the end of WW II, there was a surge of Japanese and German suicides. Refusing to accept defeat, many Commanders took their own lives.

During wartime, spies and espionage were a part of the scheme of things in plotting a war. Spies who were captured, and also officers, would commit suicide rather than risk revealing secrets while subjected to interrogation and possible torture.

Suicidal behavior could be seen during battles. An example at the Battle of Waterloo, was a soldier who placed himself in front of cannon fire, rather than take cover—in order to save the lives of fellow soldiers while losing his own.

In the charge of the Light Brigade in the Crimean War, at Gettysburg in the American Civil War at Pickett's Charge, soldiers continued to charge the enemy under odds inevitable to be fatal—similar to Custer's Last Stand. (Indian Wars) This "fighting to the last man," occurred during the Pacific Island battles in World War II, by Japanese soldiers, who set off on "banzai" suicide charges.

The struggles and stresses of warfare, said the U.S. Army, is helping push a record number of suicides. They related that the pressures of armed conflict and matters that relate, are exacting a toll on our military.

Totals of soldier suicides in 2006 were the highest in over twenty-five years. Those deaths happened even though the Army stepped up and installed new mental health programs while reorganizing old ones. These programs are designed to provide counseling and support to the military who are engaged in war in Iraq and wherever engaged to combat terrorism.

Medical teams have been shipped to the battlefield in Iraq to examine circumstances and revise programs for those who serve there, including chaplains. The suicide prevention programs already in place, are enlisting more psychiatrists and other mental health professional to instruct soldiers on how to spot problems in themselves and other soldiers. Part of the training is assuaging fears and embarrassment because of the stigma in asking for help. Some of the dread to get any kind of counseling is that doing so would ruin their military careers.

According to reports, 99 soldiers in 2007 committed suicide. Of those 99 military deaths by suicide, 30 were soldiers serving in Iraq and Afghanistan.

A fourth of these troops had a history of some form of mental health problem. Mood disorder was diagnosed previously in about twenty per-cent, such as bipolar, anxiety related disorders, including post traumatic stress disorder which is prevalent of soldiers from war in Iraq.

The engagement and involvement of soldiers in war can be traumatic and have dramatic effects afterward. Military psychiatrists attempted during the 20th century to manage syndromes and programs dealing with mental disorders. Detection and interventions and ongoing psychological treatment after deployment were being implemented. Various type screenings turned out to not be of much help on the front lines regarding effects of treatment because the postwar symptoms are mixed and chronic.

Army medical department's senior forces director believes that one in five of the soldiers in Iraq will return with symptoms of P.T.S.D. (post-traumatic-stress disorder) Their concern is that Iraq could duplicate the reslts psychologically of Vietnam. Psychiatric problems remained low, as compared to the world wars, but high numbers suffered with PTSD later on. As many as 20 per-cent, it's been warned, will return from Iraq with the disorder, this according to Captain Jennifer Berg, the chairman of psychiatric services at the Naval Medical Center in San Diego.

Captain Berg added to her statements that she believes that some of the psychological difficulties and the suicides, are connected to their direct combat experiences rather than the aftermath. Berg said, "In comparison with the conditions of chronic stress which the troops are experiencing every day. It is a combination of danger, boredom and sleep deprivation, and the knowledge that they are a long way from home."

Some of the symptoms the psychiatrists have seen range from sleep disorders, nausea and diarrhea, to anxiety and alienation and irrational anger.

One of those soldiers was Army Specialist Joseph Suell, who wrote a last letter home to his mother before committing suicide with an overdose. In the letter, he expressed a fear of being killed by an Iraqi sniper, and described the conditions and terrain he was living in . . . also, fear of his future.

In military psychiatric circles, it's generally believed that suicide rates drop or rise according to when the survival instinct "kicks in" in the war zone. During the entire Gulf War, only two suicides were reported. The unusualness of the higher rate of suicides in Iraq, compared to Korea, Vietnam, and World War II, is that this all-volunteer forces has been psychologically screened and tested for suitability. They have the benefit of combat stress briefings, and training to counter suicidal thoughts and feelings. These sessions were mandatory after a wave of suicides which demoralized the Pentagon in the late nineties.

A radio news report about U.S. Military soldiers in Iraq, from Pacifica Radio, reported this story: "There have been reports from Iraq of non-combat related deaths, and some observers speculate that many of these deaths may have been suicides. According to a recent article in the Washington Post, there have been a dozen or more suicide deaths in Iraq.

Military doctors and soldiers say part of the challenge for troops in Iraq is handling the stress of a long deployment in oven-like temperatures, rationed water and no precise knowledge of when they're going home." (end of radio report)

After the Pentagon reported the 22 soldier suicides in the war in Iraq, a retired Army Ranger was quoted, "It's statistically too high, and could by as many as 30 in Iraq." The ranger, Steve Robinson, is lobbying Congress to tell the true facts of the psychological toll of the war.

Lt. General James Peake, Army Surgeon General, made this comment, "Our leadership is heavily engaged to make sure that we are doing everything possible to take care of even that one soldier that might take his life."

The fact is, the Pentagon hasn't included in that survey the troops stationed in the U.S. Who've committed suicide following tours in Iraq. At Walter Reed Army Medical Center, two soldiers who were hospitalized there, and war vets, died by hanging themselves.

Three years ago an army study on predicted suicides was mostly overlooked until over 600 troops began being shipped out of Iraq reportedly for psychiatric reasons.

"I tried to blow my head off with my weapon and then one split-second more and I would have succeeded," a soldier said. "I mean I had the gun to my head with the safety off, with the round chambered."

Of the 25 million veterans in the United States, 1.6 million served in Afghanistan and Iraq.

One of the suicides that was reported was of Army reservist, Tim Bowman. He patrolled one of the most dangerous zones in Baghdad, called Airport Road. Tim had been home about eight months, and on Thanksgiving day, he committed suicide.

Another soldier found dead was a colonel in the U.S. Army. Ted Westhusing had taught English at the U.S. Military Academy at West Point. And, he had a family; married with three children.

Ted believed in the war in Iraq, and that it was a just war. Because he felt strongly about it, he volunteered for it. He was to serve for six months.

Col. Westhusing was found dead in his quarters at Camp Dublin in Baghdad. Only a month left to go on his tour, and he would be back with his family stateside.

During his tour in Iraq, he was the highest-ranking U.S. Soldier to die in Iraq. The Army's Criminal Investigation Command report on his death described it as: "perforating gunshot wound of the head and manner of death was suicide."

Documents by the Army's Criminal Investigation Command and Inspector General had this to say: "Something he saw in Iraq drove him to this," said an Army officer and friend. "The sum of what he saw going on drove him to take his own life." He added, "it's because he believed in duty, honor, country that he's dead."

The officer also said that, "strength of character was Ted's defining characteristic. It was unflinching integrity." It was that integrity, he said, that was also Westhusing's great flaw. "To be a true flaw, the personality has to have great strength. And that characteristic caused his downfall."

According to research, men who have served in the military are at greater risk to commit suicide than those who haven't. A war study author, Mark Kaplan, said, "Male veterans are twice as likely as their civilian counterparts to die by suicide." A professor at Portland State University, teaching on community health, he and a group of researchers gathered data on 320,000 men. Those who participated in the National Health Interview Survey, men over 18, were followed-up for a period of twelve years.

That survey revealed that soldiers in the armed forces between 1917 and 1994 were two times more likely to commit suicide than their counterparts in civilian life.

Kaplan also reported that suicide was more likely if the men had fewer duties because of health problems. Other statistics given in the study: suicides occurred more often by older men, white, better educated and married.

To accommodate the serious mental health crisis, the Department of Veteran Affairs has organized a 24-hour, National Suicide Prevention Hot-Line. The program for access to immediate psychological help will benefit all soldiers, vets as well as soldiers exiting from Iraq and Afghanistan said Jim Nicholson, Secretary of Veterans Affairs.

Washington, D.C. (March 21, 2007) a news report: Suicide Prevention Action Network today praised the U.S. House for overwhelmingly approving the Joshua Onvig Veterans S.P. Act to prevent the incidence of suicide among veterans.

The bill is named for Joshua Onvig who committed suicide in 2005. After completing an eleven month tour of duty in Iraq, Joshua came back home to Iowa where he suffered from PTSD. (post-traumatic-stress-disorder)

Speaking at the U.S. Senate, Jerry Reed, Executive Director of S.P.A.N. U.S.A., said, "Suicide is not a single illness with one true cause, it is a final outcome with multiple potential antecedents, percipients, and underlying causes.

A majority of veterans who consider suicide are not currently receiving medical care through the V.A. Therefore, family members of veterans need to recognize the warning signs for suicide and learn about services for their loved ones before it is too late." (end of quote by Jerry Reed)

A new military report sent out word that soldier suicides in 2007 were higher than they've ever been in 26 years. The report stated that more than a fourth killed themselves while serving in Iraq and Afghanistan. "Iraq was the most common deployment location for both suicides and attempts," the news report said.

Of the 99 soldier suicides, 28 served in both wars, and 71 who were not in Iraq or Afghanistan. The high rate of deaths by suicide occuring as the Pentagon was developing new mental health programs and bolstering old ones for the men and women strained to the breaking point.

Motivation for suicide that were mentioned in the military report were: relationships on the rocks or failed, financial problems and combat stress. "In addition, there was a significant relationship between suicide attempts and number of days deployed," particularly to Iraq and Afghanistan it stated. Also: "There is limited evidence to support the view that multiple deployments are a risk factor for suicide behaviors."

Up to one-fourth of the soldiers had a history of some type of mental problem. About twenty per-cent had been diagnosed with bipolar and depressive disorder; eight per-cent fell into the categories of anxiety disorder, including PTSD.

Post-traumatic-stress-disorder is linked to soldier deaths by suicide. A news story from Boston, July 25, 2007, reported that the parents of a vet back from the war in Iraq had committed suicide, sued the U.S. Government for "wrongful death," charging that their son hanged himself after the government ignored his depression.

Lance Corporal Jeffrey Lucey was discharged from the Marine Corps on August 15, 2003. He had enlisted in the Marine Reserves after graduating from high school in 1999. From a small town in central Massachusetts, Jeffrey was assigned to the 6th Transport Battalion. The 6th Motors were part of the invasion of Iraq in March 2003. In a letter to his girlfriend, Jeffrey Lucey wrote: "I have done so much immoral shit during the last month that life is never going to seem the same, and all I want is to erase the past month, pretend it didn't happen."

When Lucey returned home from the Iraqi war, he enrolled at a nearby community college in Holyoke. It was reported by the Daily Hampshire Gazette, the local newspaper, that he began showing overt signs of distress on Christmas Eve. He was having severe nightmares, and throwing-up daily. Before long, he began to drink heavily, and quit going to classes. He couldn't sleep, and suffered from hallucinations. He told his sister that he had "a rope and tree picked out."

His parents persuaded their son to see a therapist, who referred him to the Leeds VA hospital. At the hospital, he didn't want treatment out of fear that troops in his unit would hear he was "sick," but reportedly he threw a punch at one of the doctors, and at that point was involuntarily committed to the VA hospital over Memorial Day week-end and placed on suicide watch. According to his parents, they were told by a VA psychiatrist after his death that during that week-end, Lucey had threatened to kill himself. Still, the VA discharged him on Tuesday.

When their son continued to drink heavily, and acted more and more erratic, and totaled the family car, his parents took him back to the VA hospital with the hope that they would hospitalize him. The on-duty medical doctor, who wasn't a psychiatrist, made the diagnosis on his own that Jeffrey was o.k.; he could go home, that he wasn't imminently dangerous to himself or others. Seventeen days later, he found a rope, and hanged himself.

Jeffrey Lucey suffered from post-traumatic-stress-disorder. PTSD is diagnosed when you have experienced or witnessed a traumatic event that caused you to react with intense fear, helplessness, or horror, and you have had PTSD for longer than one month, and you have impaired ability to function.

Symptoms that occur within four weeks of a traumatic event may be caused by acute stress and anxiety. If it extends past a month, the diagnosis is changed to PTSD People who get treatment, counseling and medication, generally feel the symptoms lessen, but may never completely recover, struggling with PTSD for a lifetime.

Post-traumatic-stress-disorder can heighten the risk for suicide, more so if accompanied by other conditions like anxiety, substance abuse, or serious mood disorders.

Reports on soldiers and PTSD specifically comes from the U.S. Military doctors. The Iraqi war has provided heightened awareness about combat and PTSD. There's more understanding of traumas, brain injuries, and combat stress, and treatments. PTSD is the psychological damage happening in military warfare, domestic violence and child abuse.

In the course of research on PTSD, depression, and links to suicide, data revealed that during the early 1800's, Army medical doctors were evaluating soldiers with "exhaustion" after the stress of battle. Symptoms were described as "a shutting down of the mind," to escape the pain of the horrors they experienced and witnessed.

During World War I, extreme mental fatigue was diagnosed as "soldiers heart," and "the effort syndrome," Then, in WW II, the term, "shell-shock" originated, along with the expression, "combat fatigue." These were terms used to describe the effects of combat stress. There is a term in war that is called "Post-traumaatic-stress-disorder," that became a more present-day term in the Third edition of the Diagnostic and Statistical Manual of Mental Disorders (DSM) in 1980, In the current edition, DSM-IV (1994) PTSD is in a group of new stress response category in the anxiety disorder category.

PTSD, described as an anxiety disorder, develops after to a terrifying event or ordeal in which grave physical harm occurred or was threatened. Traumaatic events that could set off PYSD include violent personal assaults, natural or human-caused disasters, accidents or military combat. People with PTSD have recurrent, frightening thoughts and memories of the event, and become emotionally numb. Other symptoms can involve sleeplessness, trouble concentrating, anger and irritability, hypervigilance (constantly watching and scanning surroundings) extreme physical reactions to being touched, etc., disturbing nightmares of the disturbing event, feel detached and numb, and easily startled.

In a report from a study (2006) the New England Journal of Medicine, wrote that as many as 16 per-cent of soldiers returning home from Iraq suffered from mental problems, and major among them was PTSD. Army Surgeon General, Lt. General Kevin Kiley reported in 2007 that of 1,000 Army troops interviewed after being engaged in combat in Iraq, 30 per-cent manifested PTSD. These symptoms can emerge months, and even years afterwards. Called "delayed onset" PTSD, it makes an accurate diagnosis at discharge, a difficult gray area. Adding to the confusion, some refuse to disclose symptoms that they feel may make them look weak; for some it's distrust.

A seriosly disturbed soldier serving in Iraq shot himself while lying in his bunk in 2005. Pfc. Jason Scheuerman was one of the unusually high numbers of soldier suicides in Iraq and Afghanistan. (152) His parents persisted when the military stonewalled them about information on their son's suicide death.

What they learned from documentation and interviews, showed that Jason had seemed "out of touch with reality," and suffered with severe depression. An Army chaplain started in an interview that he had observed him "bobbing his head on the muzzle," of his gun. Sent to a military psychologist, Jason returned without treatment, and suggesting that he could be exaggerating to avoid duty.

A report from the Veterans Affairs predicted that as 5,000 vets will commit suicide within the next twelve months. This serious pronouncement comes out, claiming that the VA is negligent in providing immediate 24-hour help.

The assessment also described a laack of competently trained staff in the 1,400 clinics inspected, as well as deficient mental health screening.

Recognizing the high numbers of PTSD, the report reccomended in their advisement to the VA, that their health care facilities provide 24-hour suicide crisis intervention and mental health care by thoroughly trained staff.

Post-war findings in Finland, (a country in N. Europe) was presented at the Academy of Finland science breakfast, researcher Ville KivimAukj, described the aftermath of war, and what influence psychiatry played in shaping Finish culture following World War II. While most psychiatrists were of the opinion that soldiers returning to civilian life had adapted satisfactorily, KivinAukj expressed this adapability not to an absence of psychological problems, but rather to psychiatrists putting the responsibility for long-term problems on the soldiers themselves.

"Refusing to talk about traumatic war experiences is related to a deep-seated culture of shame and very limited resources for veterans to express their traumas," the researcher said at the breakfast. KivinAukj went on to say, "War psychiatry had a profound impact on the creation of the culture. Even though the restrictive and stigmatizing aspects of war psychiatry might seem repulsive, it did establish a certain type of reality, defined possibilities for the existence of soldiers and veterans, and created tension between traumatic war experiences and the cultural forms of expressing them."

One of the unlikely candidates for suicide was Admiral Jeremy Boorda, Chief of Naval Operations. He was an admiral of the United States Navy and the 25th Chief of Naval Operations.

Admiral Boorda died May 16, 1996 of a self-inflicted gunshot wound to the chest. The explanation given in the official report said that he was depressed over a news media investigation into valor enhancements that he wore on his Navy Achievement Medal and a Navy Commendation Medal (small brass v's, signifying valor in combat), which the media report claimed Boorda wasn't entitled to wear.

However, Boorda's commander in Vietnam, Admiral Elmo Zumwalt, indicated that the medals were authorized, and was doing nothing wrong in wearing them. One of Admiral Boorda's sons requested a review of the Admiral's service record. The Board for Correction of Naval Records, the highest arbiter of whether or not Boorda was entitled to wear the combat v on both medals, determined that he was not.

Boorda began in an "enlisted-to-officer" commission program in the early 1960;s. It was known as the Integration Program and was designed to provide an opportunity for enlisted personnel who possessed outstanding qualifications and motivation for a naval career to obtain a commission.

Admiral Boorda was the first CNO to have risen out of the ranks of the enlisted. Admiral Boorda reestablished the historic program, calling it "Seaman to Admiral," as part of a STA-21 for young sailors to earn their commission and become naval officers. Admiral Boorda felt that, "People should have the opportunity to excel, and be all they can be, even if they don't get a perfect or traditional start."

Violent deaths are a part of war. Violence is a by-product of warfare. "Killing the opponents soldiers is not the goal of warfare in and of itself, although inflicting casualties on the enemy is one means of achieving the purpose of war," said Charles P. McDowell, PhD. A researcher of war, he continued, "The objective of combat is to reduce the enemy's ability to wage war and thereby hasten the defeat of his political leadership.

Within the military, the job of inflicting casualties is limited to certain specialties; the remainder of the military organization provides support . . .

all members of the military learn to kill when they go through basic combat skills and military discipline."

In an armed conflict, the military is bounded by law, treaty and custom regarding when, where, and how the killing is done. Any behavior that breaches this understood code of professional soldiers, is looked upon with disdain.

Suicide, and also murder, go outside of these boundaries of acceptable military conduct. Although deaths by suicide or murder isn't the norm, the military is not free of these tragedies. It is a recorded fact, that suicide ranks third as the cause of death among soldiers, who are active in the military.

At Fort Hood, Texas, III Corps lost nine soldiers to suicide. Unfortunately, the stigma of seeking help for being, "mental," stops opportunities for counsel and support, that could save their lives.

Army officials at Fort Bliss in Texas, reported the suicide of 19 year-old Spc. John R. Fish. He wandered off from a desert training range and was found nearby with a single, self-inflicted gunshot wound to the head.

He was only reported missing when he didn't show up for the morning roll call. Army officials later discovered a note on his bunk that read, "I have some things to take care of. I won't be coming back."

Spc. Fish was at Fort Bliss for training. He was an ammunitions specialist with the 41st Fires Brigade, a field artillery unit based at Fort Hood. He had left that morning wearing his camouflage uniform and carrying a squad automatic weapon. It was in the Army's report that his weapon was next to his body.

The escalating number of soldier suicides has caused alarm at the Pentagon said a Lt. Colonel. Cameron Ritchie, a psychiatrist at the Army's Uniformed Services University of the Health Sciences in Bethesda, Maryland, is involved in investigating the soldier suicides in Iraq. He questions, "Is there something different going on in Iraq that we really need to pay attention to?"

Another casualty of suicide was Army private Corey Small, from a colonial town near the battlefield of Gettysburg. Not a large town, the story of how Corey died in June, 2004, was soon known by people in his home town. "We're a small community, and news travels fast," said Mayor Keith Hoffman. The death was a tragedy to his community and his family. He had a wife and a four year-old son. There was a different feeling with a few members of the local American Legion Chapter in Lake Meade. They want to discontinue plans to name that post after Small.

One of the Pentagon's top doctors reportedly made the statement that suicide has become such a priority that the Army sent an assessment team to Iraq last year to investigate. In spite of these efforts, and offers of more counseling for troops returning home after war, several soldiers in Fort Bragg, North Carolina, committed murder and suicide.

In November of 2002, authorities said that four Fort Bragg soldiers killed their wives in June and July, 2002. Two of the men committed suicide and the other two were charged with murder. Three of those cases involved Special Operations soldiers who had served in Afghanistan. After the murders, the military announced that soldiers would be screened for psychological problems before returning stateside.

American veterans go all the way back to the American Civil War, 1861-1865. From The Los Angeles Times, June 04, 1900: "An ex-confederate, Louis Doolittle, old and now crippled, who fought in the Confederate Army during the Civil War, committed suicide in his room in the Olive Tree Inn, a lodging house on Twenty-Third Street. A letter was found in his pocket addressed to a Mrs. M.M. Smith of Brooklyn."

Erwin Rommel, the German general in WW II, had the nick-name of "the Desert Fox." He was commended for bravery and earned the Iron Cross. The name "Desert Fox" came about because of his traversing about in the North Africa Theater. Rommel and his Atrike Corps were defeated by the British, and forced to surrender, trapped between British and American forces.

Called back to Germany, Rommel assisted in the defense against the approaching invasion. Wounded in an attack, he was hospitalized. While in the hospital, it was rumored that he was involved in a plot to assassinate Adolph Hitler. At that point, it was said that he was given a choice of suicide or public execution for treason. The public execution would include his family. Rommel committed suicide, although news report said that he died from his wounds in the hospital.

This next and final story is about a 24 year-old Marine who was a prisoner of war in Vietnam. (S.E. Asia in E. Indochina, U.S. Involved in war when North and South divided, 1954-1976) While a P.O.W. of the Vietcong, the VC promised him that he could have his freedom, be released only if he would agree to become a leader. He believed that he would also escape being tortured, and he agreed to "be a leader." Only, his duties involved betraying his buddies. He participated in "Manchurian-type brainwashing techniques" on fellow soldiers. The Vietcong didn't only break the promise to release him, but smashed his hope, too. When finally he realized that he wouldn't be released after all, he lay on his cot, sucking his thumb. Soon after, he died.

Chapter Five

Divine Intervention

A divine intervention by direct or indirect means is always a wonder, a marvel—but never our call—it's God's.

This first story came out of Oklahoma. Zack Dunlap, 21, was in an ATV accident and sustained a severe head injury. His family said that the church signs all over the town of Frederick, appealed to everyone to pray for Zack Dunlap.

Zack's injury was so severe, and even brain-dead, that he was being prepped for an organ donation when he suddenly grabbed his nurse's arm.

Zack's family believed it, "a miracle," saying that one moment they're telling him goodbye, and the next, being told he's come back to life.

Betsy Randolph, an Oklahoma state trooper said, "During this time, while the nurse was prepping his body for organ transplant, he grabbed her arm." It was reported that his uncle, James Bradford, said, "God came down and gave him a miracle. I believe that with all my heart."

Zach's next-door neighbor and friend, was of the belief, "I think it's the result of people praying in this town, and committing him to the Lord. I believe God has a purpose for his life."

#

In Scotland, a legendary cyclist, Graemo Obree, also experienced a Divine Intervention. Obree, from a place called, Irving Ayrshire, was known in those parts as, "the Flying Scot." He won first place in a world tour event two years in a row. He achieved this in the early 90's on a bike that he built with tubes from a BMX, and ball-bearings from a washing machine.

Doctors are in agreement that he was suffering from severe bipolar disorder since the age of 19. Obree, 37, said he has fought with manic depression all his life. The cyclist revealed that he's attempted suicide more than once since he was a teen-ager.

On the day he tried to hang himself, he said he was "dreadfully depressed to the point of thinking about suicide. I cycled seven miles to the stables—and that was it, I just hung myself."

Obree was hanging from one of the rafters in the barn, when a teen-age girl found him. "If she had arrived just one minute later, then I would have been dead. That was how close I was." A divine intervention.

#

In 2004, a country-western singer by the name of Mindy McReady was arrested and charged with one count of prescription drugs found. She was fined $4,000 (dollars) after pleading guilty, and was sentenced to three years supervised probation and ordered to perform 200 hours of community service.

Mindy McReady's debut album, in 1996, was "Ten Thousand Angels," and went gold a year later. In 2002, Capital Records dropped her, saying that her records weren't selling like before.

Several months after her arrest in 2004, she was arrested again, this time for drunk driving. And things got worse, as her behavior got more self-destructive.

The same year, she was violently beaten and almost strangled to death by her boyfriend, who she'd just broken—up with. Hospitalized and released, Mindy went into seclusion. Not long after, she made an attempt on her life by overdosing.

Mindy later set the record straight, and said she wasn't trying to kill herself, that it was actually a "divine intervention, God's way of trying to get my attention and telling me that I'm supposed to be out there singing and entertaining."

#

When lost her brother to a disease that she believed God could have healed, she began to question God because she felt that her "prayers weren't answered." In her grief, she fell into a deep depression and even attempted to end her life.

"A black depressive cloud hung over my head, and I was put on anti-depressants. I experienced some resentment towards my Heavenly Father for not coming to my brother's aid. He could have healed him so easily. Why didn't He? He had lived a painful, difficult life.

While in the depths of depression, I made an attempt to take my own life by swallowing eight tablets, which I was told should have killed me if they had been the right type of tablets. I thank God now that they weren't.

During my enforced one week stay in the psychiatric section of a local hospital, I had time to ponder issues in my life on a deep level. It wasn't up to me to question God about why He hadn't healed my brother. God in His supreme wisdom always knows what is best for a person. I know now that God showed compassion for my brother in his illness."

#

Thomas was successful and prosperous in the world of business, but still felt empty inside, void of meaning in his life. After enduring years of depression and pain, Thomas tried to take his own life. "I was a working professional in the medical field with twenty years of experience at two New York hospital centers. I had all the material possessions that people seek. I had all the bells and whistles that the secular world strives for, at least I thought so at the time. To top it all off, I had a caring relationship with a great lady by the name of Connie.

Yet, there was something missing in my life—a void, an aching hollowness, a lack of completeness, a lack of meaningful purpose for my existence that I just could not find or fill. Material possessions, drugs, alcohol, and switching relationships—these pursuits would not satisfy me for any length of time. They always left me coming up short. Nothing could make me feel complete.

I did not understand at the time that my life needed eternal purpose. I thought I had achieved my purpose—after all, I had succeeded at the "Great American Dream." I thought life was just about having fun and meeting my needs. As much as Connie pleaded with me to stop my destructive behavior, I could not. Connie cared so much for me, but could not watch me kill myself one drink at a time. I was blind to it all. I robbed her of health and peace. I was so selfish and self-seeking and ended up hurting the very one who meant the world to me. I loved Connie and she loved me, but I didn't love myself enough to change. Something dramatic was about to happen.

The darkness in my soul seemed to grow and I watched it overpower me. With this and a combination of alcohol and a bankrupt spirit, I turned away from the last positive thing in my life. I decided that death was the only answer for me—the only way to escape the despair I was in, to hopefully end the pain I was causing myself and those who loved me most.

I devised a plan, a fool-proof plan that would be successful to its very ending. I examined it thoroughly—inside out, forward and backwards. 'A perfect suicide,' my darkened mind rationalized. 'A blaze of glory.' I set the stage during the time when the fewest amount of important people would be walking around to possibly get hurt—one o' clock in the morning to be exact. I planned the location, I knew where the police would be firing from—a backdrop of an embankment. I was sort of in a soup bowl. I did not want any stray bullets possible, harming anyone else. No one was to be hurt but me. The stage was finally set for my final exit.

I found the police by calling 911. I said, "There is a crazy person running around the complex with a gun." I was living in W. Knoxville at the time, and had mapped out my plan in the field in front of the complex.

On that fateful night, September 16, 2005, I painted a bull's eye on my chest. My purpose for doing so, was to send a message that would inform my sister that this was a planned suicide. I did not notify anyone of what I was about to do. No last minute phone calls. This was not a cry for help. I was prepared to die.

When the police arrived, I was gazing straight up at the sky, transfixed on this one, lone star in the cold, dark sky. I prayed upon that star with all my heart. I prayed that this ordeal would be over quickly and as painlessly as possible. I also prayed that Connie and my sister, Katty, would forgive me for what I was about to do. Then I asked God for forgiveness.

The police arrived as expected, with all the noise of bullhorns and shouting going on, blinding lights pointing in my direction. It was pretty surreal. My heart was pounding, but there was no turning back now.

The life and death tension was building up to an insane crescendo. It was time to force them to shoot. It was time to reach for my BB pistol. My plan was about to be fully executed.

When I reached for the pistol, six officers shot at me. They shot a combined total of 28 times, yet only one bullet hit me! It hit me with such force it knocked me off my feet. Lying there on the ground waiting to die—blood everywhere—I knew my miserable life was going to be over shortly. Everything was a hazy blur after that.

I have heard all the explanations. Poor shooting skills, luck, bad lights, nerves, conscience and other rationalities. However, no one can convince me otherwise—I know the Lord was standing in front of me, and forgiving me, while I could not forgive myself.

I was convicted, rightly so, and spent the next 18 months in jail for felony aggravated assault and reckless endangerment. In jail I had time to ponder my life—my poor decisions, the people I hurt, my reason for being so selfish.

It was there in my tiny cell that God began to do deep, emotional surgery on me. The Spirit of the living God began to draw me to Jesus Christ in a way I had never known. He redeemed me, causing me to be spiritually born again as John 3:3 speaks of.

#

A divine intervention can happen by God showing us "a sign." Lynn Tolson related that her first steps toward recovery began when she asked for help. She was quoted as saying, "I was driving about aimlessly after a suicide attempt. I was overwhelmed with pain. It was not the physical pain of a fractured limb, but the psychic pain of a fractured soul. As I had done before, I prayed aloud: 'God, tell me what to do and show me where to go. God, show me a sign!

I can describe what happened next as divine intervention. I say a sign at a house converted into an office: Family Counseling Center. Even as I cried, I knocked at the door, and was greeted by a woman naamaed Karen. She was a counselor there, and my therapeutic relationship began that day. After our first session, I moved from feeling despair to a sense of hope."

#

This is a short and twisted tale that horrifies and redeems with God's good grace. According to the singer, Laura Love, at the age of twelve—at the request of her mother—began looking for a rope to hang herself. Before putting her head in the noose, her mother asked her to hang the family cat, Sugar Plum, first. The evil deed done—Laura ran from the scene in tears. It was later recalled by Laura that it was her "inability to tie a good knot, my haste and Sugar Plum's good luck," and her divine intervention that prevented the twisted murder/suicide that day.

#

A story from the Globe, out of Toronto, Canada. A suicidal man decided to terrorize his estranged wife by jumping off an overpass with their five year-old daughter.

It happened at an overpass in Canada's Highway 401. The father was killed on impact, but a divine intervention for the child.

"This guy was a loaded missile. He was going to kill himself and he was going to take his daughter to punish his wife for whatever he thought she had done wrong in the relationship," Inspector Brian O'Conner said at a news briefing on the jump.

"The fact that the little girl wasn't hit by a car is a miracle," he added.

And although the little girl had internal bleeding from falling onto the highway, no bones were broken. She was airlifted and taken to The Hospital For Sick Children where she was expected to have a good recovery.

Police stated that the man left his wife a suicide note. They said he went to his wife's house in the late afternoon to pick up his daughter. It wasn't long before he began calling his wife, threatening to kill himself and their daughter.

"He continued to call his wife while he had the daughter in what amounts to psychological torture by telling her, "I'm going to kill myself, I'm going to kill my daughter," said Inspector O' Conner.

His wife notified police about her husband's threats, and they immediately began a desperate search while at the same time negotiating with him over his cell phone. By the time police were able to trace his cell phone signal, they were on the bridge. Just before 6:00 p.m., police were getting calls that a man was dangling a girl over the overpass in North Toronto.

There were officers on the bridge, but had no chance to talk with him before he jumped. "He never acknowledged the officers on the bridge. He stayed on the cell phone, and with his five year-old daughter, he just went over," Inspector O' Conner said.

Witnesses reportedly said that the man threw his daughter over the bridge and then jumped. Cars typically cross at more than 100 kilometers an hour on the highway and police didn't have time to stop traffic. The Inspector added, "The fact that the little girl wasn't hit by a car is a miracle."

#

The following is an open testimony of a Christian, Ed Coit: "I am a suicide survivor. I am also a Christian. My testimony explains how anyone, especially people of faith, can survive or help others.

My father, a career soldier, committed suicide with an overdose of prescription medicine taken in conjunction with alcohol. Alcohol is a depressant that exacerbates suicidal tendencies in those who are prone to such self-destructive acts. I was sixteen years old at the time. I was wrongly ashamed of my father's suicide for most of my life. In fact, that feeling of shame is one of the great regrets of my time. With the combination of drugs and alcohol, my dad might not have ever intended to take his life. It could have been an accident. There was no suicide note. He had no previous declaration of intent to commit suicide. The answers to that mystery we will never know. Still, officially his death certificate declared it a suicide.

Some twenty years after my father's death I had to cope with multiple suicide attempts by my brother. He had a lot close calls. More than once death was knocking at his door. After every attempt he would be grateful for his life. But then he would get depressed and regress . . . he'd attempt it (suicide) again and again.

My brother is a Viet Nam veteran. He suffers from post-traumatic-stress-disorder. PTSD. Depression is a consequence of PTSD. He came to terms with his mental illness and sought treatment. I have no doubt that treatments, medication, and prayer are what saved his life. It has allowed him to live a mostly productive life, although he still struggles with his illness. Treatment, medication and prayer are the difference between my brother and my father. Our dad had none of these and, of course, he died.

The reality is that in severe cases of mental illness, nothing short of divine intervention can save a suicidal person."

#

JESUS CHRIST IS MANKIND'S DIVINE INTERVENTION

Since Adam we are all under the condition of sin. "By one man sin entered the world, and death by sin; and so death passed upon all men, for that all have sinned." Romans 5:12. But, God in his love and mercy, provided a way, a gift, to counteract the transgression of Adam and Eve that resulted. "The wages of sin is death; but the gift of God is eternal life." Romans 6:23. And in 1 John 5:11, "This if the record, that God has given to us eternal life, and this life is in His Son."

Mankind's original sin and God's regeneration to man are reborn at the cross. The cross is how we get our life back from a spiritual death. "I am crucified with Christ: nevertheless I live; yet not I, but Christ liveth in me: and the life which I now live in the flesh, I live by the faith of the Son of God, who loved me, and gave himself for me." Galatians 2:20.

A spiritual renewal of our mind and soul takes place as we accept God's grace. We are then free, liberated, not to walk about in condemnation—but in God's love that quickens our spirit.

"God, who is rich in mercy, for his great love wherewith He loved us, even when we were dead in sins, hath quickened us together with Christ." Ephesians 2:4,5.

So, we have salvation by faith, from spiritual death to eternal life. "Being born again, not of corruptible seed, but of incorruptible, by the word of God, which liveth and abideth forever." 1 Peter 1:23. We all have access by faith to be reconciled to God. Colossians 1:20: "And, having made peace through the blood of his cross, by him to reconcile all things unto himself; by him, I say, whether they be things on earth, or things in Heaven."

Sometimes in life we drop down into despair, thinking that nothing can be done about it. It is an ordinary human trait, but Jesus understands this, he says to us: "Arise and do the next thing." There is no growth without failure. Build failure into the learning curve—it's part of it. God said He would be there for us and direct our path.

"Be of good courage, and he shall strengthen your heart, all ye that hope in the Lord." Psalm 31:24.

Chapter Six

Cultural Divides—On Acts Of Suicide

In some cultures to speak of suicide is taboo. In the United States—until recently—it was considered a crime. And in India, there was a time when women were expected to burn themselves on a funeral pyre after the death of their husbands.

EGYPT

In Egypt, suicide was seen as a way to escape what they perceive as an unbearable situation. During World War II it was considered an honor to be a Japanese Kamikaze pilot.

And in other cultures, however, the act of suicide has been condemned or made illegal. In ancient \Rome, governments were disapproving of suicide when the state stood to lose resources like soldiers or slaves. Suicide was strictly forbidden by Judaism unless about to be captured by the enemy, as in the suicides at Masada.

By the Middle Ages, the Roman Catholic Church prohibited the burial of one who committed suicide in consecrated ground. If you committed suicide under English law, it was a crime punishable by the forfeiture of belongings and property to the government unless one was insane or gravely ill.

CHINA.

Chinese culture throughout history has been ambivalent concerning the act of suicide. It is commonly spoken of, allowed and even sanctioned. It is often done to escape shame or dishonor or tragedy, especially when under strong coercion. Ritual suicide is common in Chinese culture, generally related to political protest.

In China's traditional culture, moral systems prevail and suicide is forbidden or is looked upon disfavorably. Suicide has been linked with gender in Chinese culture. In the past, and in present day China it's not uncommon for females committing suicide because of adversity and contributing condemning attitude of family members.

In some instances in Chinese culture suicide was even given an air of trance-like glamor. Stories become legend of lovers joined in death who for various reasons couldn't be together in life. The Butterfly lovers is one example' and Pan Yu-An and Su-Qi, in "A Dream of Red Mansions," one of the four great works of Chinese literature.

In modern day China the suicide rate among females is uncommonly high, and is in fact the highest in the world. Suicide is also common in rural areas where distance puts them at a disadvantage for available help.

INDIA

In Indian culture their view is similar to current Asian cultures of China and Japan. India has also taken an ambivalent attitude on suicide. Treated as a common occurrence during India's history, suicide has been issued only passing disfavor. Ritual suicide, particularly in the form of political protest, is not an unusual occurrence in India. Warrior codes in place that allowed it, or evev as a bent religious or philosophical view. Examples of this are reputed Kings and other notable figures.

The religions of India, such as Buddhism, Hinduism, and Sikkhism, have in the past opposed suicide, with the exception of extraordinary circumstance. The Buddhist and Hindu monks were known to carry out the custom of sallekhona, where starvation ended as suicide, which was used to pervert undue decision making. In the Indian Independence movement, when freedom fighters like Mahatma Gandhi would pronounce—"fast unto death," (starvation)

Another custom, done for similar reasons, was self-immolation, where Hindu monks would enter their own funeral pyre at the end of their lives as a type of religious rite.

As in other East Asia cultures, "death before dishonor," was a creed amongst the warrior breed, or Kshatriya, and therefore military or martial suicide was allowed if defeat was inevitable, which was the case of Rajput warriors, who would ride out to meet death when a siege was doomed, while their women would immolate themselves to escape molestation and rape, or being captured by dishonorable enemies like the Arab, Central Asian and Persian raiders of medieval times. This custom was called Jauhar.

It is well recorded that Indian warrior divisions such as Gurklas, Sardars and Rajputs gave their lives to further a battle. A number of them gained notable attention from the British, and from the Japanese during World War II because of their un-reluctance to die in battle for honor.

An extreme example of immolation in only some parts of India, involves an interpretation of select ancient philosophical texts, resulting in the practice of sati,. This was when a woman would immolate herself to join her husband in death, but the custom was abused, with women being forced into suicide by their local communities who shirk the duty of providing resources to widows.

SWEDEN

In Sweden, it has come to the attention of researchers that reindeer herders in the far north of the country were more at risk of committing suicide than other Swedes. Their study of the Sami, the people living in the far north of Scandinavia, has revealed the reasons behind this, according to Swedish radio.

"I can definitely imagine that life as a reindeer herder could be a factor," said herder, Ola Hanersk, a friend of a fellow herder who took his life, from the village of Porjus.

Researchers found that it was frequently young men who worked long days on snow mobiles, driving monotonous and endless distances it seemed. Another contributing factor they think, is the low salary they received which did little to off-set the rigors of boredom.

Doctors in Sweden can have suicidal thoughts, too. According to a local newspaper there, "nearly one-third of Sweden's doctors have considered suicide. Along with that, harassment and bullying are a part of their work environment. St Karolindka University Hospital a study was done, and results were based on the answers of 1,092 doctors.

"Naturally, this is serious," said Ann Fridner, researcher and project leader.: But, I'm not surprised. Unfortunately, it's the same pattern in the whole of the western world."

The university study also confirmed that doctors as a profession, are at an increased risk of suicide. Based on the study, one in three doctors answered that at some point they had suicidal thoughts.

RUSSIA

It's interesting to note that more people die in Russia by killing themselves than in war. Russian journalist reported in the 1860's, based on statistical data, that the suicide rate was increasing in all European countries: "Suicide is as old as humanity itself . . . but in no other epoch in human history has it been as widespread as in our enlightened and humane nineteenth century. Suicide has now become a kind of epidemic disease and furthermore a chronic disease claiming thousands of victims among the populations of all the civilized countries of Europe." Russia, as research suggests, is considered more backward as compared to other western European countries—had recently caught up with the West where suicide is concerned.

Regional data records that while numbers of suicides were generally low in southern Russia, in 1989 suicide deaths were highest in the eastern ethnic and in southeast Russia. Research indicates that suicide numbers may have been affected by societal changes of a new era. The act of suicide and society's view of it in Russia during the Communist period becoming more common among all the social classes and geographical as well.

NETHERLANDS

The open-minded culture and dismissal of religion in the Netherlands over the latter part of the 20th century contributed to the openness toward self-killing. This social environment allowed for liberal laws to be passed through parliament, legalizing euthanasia in 2001. The past few decades have seen "the right to die" on the same footing with a widely recognized right to live view. When religion declined, it changed society's attitude about suicide to the extent old, traditional views which strongly condemned it, now receded into the background.

JAPAN

Japan's cultural view towards the act of suicide is similar to China and India—tolerant in comparison to American and European cultures. A difference, however, due to recent events in Japan because of the highest rates of suicide in the world among its young people. It has forced the Japanese government to take a more serious look of suicide as a problem that needs solutions.

Traditionally, suicide has been a means to an end to maintain the family honor, especially a ritual self-disemboweling known as Seppraku that was in common use in Feudal Japan, and while the tradition mostly faded out with the demise of the Samai and the beginning of a western style society, many Japanese young people still perceive suicide as a way to avoid bringing shame and dishonor to family. In the early 21st century 30,000 Japanese became suicide statistics every year.

The act of Kamikaze—thought to belong to Japanese culture—is a myth. In fact, it was a tactic devised during the second World War by the Japanese air force and was used neither prior or after the war. The term "Kamikaze' has no significance in Japanese, other than meaning "godly wind," which originated following two storms that protected Japan from invasion by destroying the enemy fleets of Kublai Khan from Mongolia in the 13th century.

MEXICO

Although it is true worldwide, that thousands of people are killed every year from vigilante beatings, police repression, gang violence and war, the most dominant form of death is suicide. According to the World Health Organization, over one million people die each year from "self-inflicted violence," or almost twice those who die from homicide and more than twice those who die in wars.

Usually, in most cultures, suicide numbers go up with passing age, but in recent years, there has been evidence of increasing occurrence in youth, including in Latin America where the rate of suicide deaths has risen sharply in the past decade.

Since the time of Emile Durkheim's, On Suicide, in 1897, showed that suicide was present in all cultures and could not be reduced to simple attributes, but stemmed from a lack of group identification, and a system of morality. In studies of death, the rituals and relations to national identity are well knownm, especially in Mexico, although in Mexico its rarely written about or mentioned.

According to W. H.O., suicide goes unreported by as much as 40 per-cent. The reason for this may be because of various cultural and social causes. The Catholic Church believe suicide is a sin. To avoid embarrassment a suicide may be reported as a heart attack. Or it may be difficult to detect as a suicide. Traffic accidents, for example, is the most frequent cause of death for 10 to 19 year-olds in Mexico, yet, running into traffic is also mentioned in studies from the U.S. Similar vague uncertainties of a death occur in cases of overdose or electrecution. Suspicions of a violent, including suicide, leads to an investigation by the Public Prosecutor's Office to decide whether the death was assisted, encouraging doctors to record possible suicides as accidents.

Mexico's national government recently reported that over the past fifteen years Mexico had the 6th fastest growth rate for suicide in the world. (Secretaria de Salud, 2006)

Research shows that street involved youth are especially at risk, presenting high suicidal ideation, a greater number of suicide attempts and higher numbers of deaths than the general population.

Drug dependency and alcohol abuse are extensive, psychological problems and evidence of self-destructive behavior.

SUICIDE FACTS IN IRELAND AND UK

In the UK and Ireland, more than 6,000 people a year commit suicide. That's more than twice the number killed in automobile accidents; twelve times the number of deaths by homicide. In England and Wales it is estimated that as many as 140,000 people attempt suicide in a twelve month period. 5,905 in the UK, 378 suicides in the republic of Ireland in 1996. One suicide every 84 minutes in UK and Ireland. 75 per-cent of suicides are by males 785 suicides by young people in UK and Ireland—2 per day. Suicide accounts for 205 of all deaths by young people. The rate of attempted suicides is rising, a 50 per-cent increase since 1990. The suicide attempts by young men has doubled since 1985.

REPUBLIC OF IRELAND

In the Republic of Ireland there has been a 24 per-cent increase in the number of people committing suicide since 1985. The rate for males was approximately 22 per-cent, for females the rate was approximaately 5 per 100,000 population. For all of the Republic of Ireland the suicide rate was 13 out of 100,000 in 1996.

SCOTLAND

Suicide statistics in Scotland—845 in 1996: 620 males and 225 females. The Scottish suicide rate was approximately 20 out of 100,000. The suicide rate for males was 30, and for females it was 10 for 100,000 population.

There has been a 12 per-cent increase in number of suicides since 1982 in Scotland.

CANADA

Canada and the United States have similar suicide rates—Canada's historically a little higher. Each year in Canada about 3,800 suicides are recorded.

OTHER COUNTRIES

Suicide rates in other countries include Latvia with the highest number of people killing themselves, (42.5 per 100,000, Lithuania (35.9) Countries with the lowest suicide rates include Guatemala (0.5), the Philippines (0.5), Albania (1.4), the Dominican Republic (2.1), and Armenia (2.3). It is, however, difficult to make reliable comparisons because of the errors in official reporting of suicides, and different systems on certifying causes.

METHODS

How people carry out their own suicide varies from culture to culture, however, hanging is the leading method of suicide all over the world. In the United States, about 60 poer-cent of all suicides are committed by firearms. Overdoses and poisoning to end their lives: 18 per-cent in the U.S. Researchers conclude that not all automobile accidents ae reported accurately, and that a small percent are actually suicides. Only about 20 per-cent of the people who commit suicide leave suicide notes.

"WELL, DOC, THIS DIDN'T SOLVE A THING—THEY END UP **CHALK FIGURES**, AND **VIOLENCE** LIVES ON!"

Chapter Seven

Murder/Suicide

According to medical studies, between 1,000 and 1,500 deaths every year in the United States are murder/suicide. Research data obtained from the VPC (Violence Policy Center) shows that, in the first half of 2001, there were 662 murder/suicide deaths, of which 293 were suicides and 369 were homicides.

Research reveals that most murderers in murder/suicides are male. In the information gathered here, 90.4 per-cent of the offenders were male.

PENNSYLVANIA: In April, David O' Kon waited for his wife who lived with her parents since their separation. When she arrived he shot Marisa Rose O' Kon once in the hand, and twice in the head. After he murdered his wife, he then committed suicide with the gun he brought. Their two year-old daughter was not injured. The couple was pronounced dead at the scene, despite efforts to revive them.

What is usually the case in murder/suicide is a relationship falling apart between partners, with the man killing his wife or girlfriend. Murder/suicide is taking place more and more. A medical professional states, "because many murder/suicides results in the death or injury of family members and sometimes mass murder, they cause countless additional mortality, family trauma, and disruption of communities." It's these crimes, the offender murders his intended victims—spouses, lover, family or strangers fefore killing himself.

CALIFORNIA: Shane Brad, a 39 year-old man with a history of violence, shot and killed his nine month pregnant wife, before turning the gun on himself. The year before, Una, his wife, had filed for a temporary restraining order requiring her husband to refrain from abusing or harassing her. Una's two teen-age daughters who witnessed the murder/suicide, told police that after the couple argued hotly, Shane shot his wife in the face and chest, then shot himself in the head. Fairfield Police Sgr. John Dugan stated, "It doesn't get much worse than shooting a pregnant woman."

This type of killing represents one-half to three-fourths of all murder/suicides in the United States. It usually involves a man between the ages of 18 to 60 year-olds who becomes jealous and suspicions of a wife or girlfriend's infidelity, becomes enraged and murders her, then himself. Often, the children are also killed who belong to the intimate couple.

TEXAS: Lucio Franco Sr., 24, shot his wife and family with a shotgun before killing himself. Each of the family members, wife, Maria, 21, and the children, Lucio, Jr. 5; Diana, 4;, Juana, 2; and Issac only nine months old was shot at close range. Investigators believe that domestic discord and even economic problems played a role in the incident.

MAINE: Harold "Bones" Gray, 68, shot and killed his wife, Christine Gray, 24, and her sister, 19, before he then shot himself. The Gray's had been married for four years, but were separated and in the process of getting a divorce. Christine Gray had taken out a proection order on her husband in November, 2000. He was arrested for violation of that order in January, 2001. All three were dead at the scene.

SOUTH CAROLINA; In June, the bodies of Carolina Blaackwood, 26, and her esranged husband were found in Rose Hill State Park. Mark Blackwood, 29, had shot his wife twice, and then shot himself, committing this murder/suicide. Relatives said the Blackwoods were struggling with financial troubles and infidelity. Mark Blackwood had threatened to kill himself the week before the shooting.

CONNECCTICUT: In May, 39 year-old Zaachary Da Costa, a massenary contractor who had been hired by a local police officer, Sergant Le Rose, to perform some work, shot and killed his ex-girlfriend, 40 year-old Francesca Benedetto, inside the officer's Danbury home. Ms. Benedeto died of multiple gunshot wounds. Police specujlated that Mr. Da Costa believed that Ms. Benedetto was having a relationship with Sergeant Le Rose. The bodies were found in the master bedroom after the Le Rose family returned home after a christening

An intimate partner or acquantance is describe as a girlfriend/boyfriend, spouse, or an ex-spouse. Most murder/suicides happen in the home of the offender and/or victim, and is the most likely place for a murder/suicide to happen.

A few of the cases pf murder/suicide involved active and inactive police officers. Some stories were reported that the gun used was the law officer's own service weapon. It's been estimated twice as many police officers commit suicide than are killed in the line of duty. Studies that compare suicide rates show that law enforcement suicide rates exceed rates for both the general population and age/gender matched groups.

NEW YORK: Finbar Mahon, a New York City police officer, killed his girlfriend and then committed suicide with his service revolver inside their Queens apartment. A note found in Mahon's pocket revealed his guilt and despair over having fallen in love with another woman. Officer Mahon, a 13 year veteran, was a forensic expert who trained fellow officers at the NYPD Bronx shooting range.

The majority of people think of suicide as a lone, solitary act that affects this one individual. But the effects and damage go far beyond the murderer. Family, often the ones killed, friends, siblings, neighbors and even children are included in this murderous act.

Domestic violence is associated with a very high number of murder/suicides. One solution to stop domestic killings, or an avenue of intervention would be legislation, and more programs made available regarding family and spiritual roots that teach control, caring and protecting a loved one—not murdering them.

The domestic violence fatality reviews of the case of the Charan Investigation took place on January 15, 1990. Joseph Charan had sought the support of various government agencies for a period of 15 months prior to deaths. Veena had been separated from Joseph and was awarded custody of their nine year-old son. During the 15 months preceding her death she made numerous reports to the police. Immediately prior to her murder, Joseph was arrested for felony wife beating and malicious mischief. As a result of his conviction for this offense Joseph received a 12 month suspended jail sentence. He was put on probation through the Adult Probation Department with the following three conditions: 1.) domestic violence course 2.) stay away order, and 3.) 30 days of jail, of which he was given 4 days, the remainder to be served in the Sheriff's Work Alternative program. Veena Charan obtained a restraining order on several occasions. He also attempted to kidnap his son at his son's school. It was at the school that Mr. Charan killed his wife in front of school teachers and school children before committing suicide.

Apart from the communication between the SFPD and the D.A',s office, there was little communication among the multiple agencies which had contact with Veena Charan. The review committee of San Francisco called for centralization of information and better coordination. These are excerpts from that investigation: Based on the incident reports involving Joseph Charan and other family members received at the hands of Joseph Charan to be serious. Specifically, the report finds that 'had the investigator looked at the pattern of violence established by Mr. Charan and presented the information to the D.A.'s office, stronger measures and responses to the situation may have prevented Joseph Charan from continuing the escalation of violence that led to the murder/suicide.

Based on the felony protocol of the D.A.'s Office, prior history was one of the factors taken into consideration concerning re-booking. If the Assistant D.A. Had access to the same information the Commission did, the re-booking charges may have been different.

A man and woman were found shot inside their car, and later died—a murder/suicide. Someone nearby saw two people arguing in the car. The woman, said that a lady was in the driver's sat, and the man was in the passenger seat. Bethlehem Police said that the report states: "The witness said she saw the woman attempt to exit the car, but the man pulled her back by her hair. The two struggled. The man then held his wife down on his lap and shot her," according to the witness. The man then committed suicide. The death of Carmen Leguilou, 39, was ruled a homicide, said Lehigh County Coroner, Scott Grim. Jerry Leguilou, 39, died of self-inflicted gunshot wounds, Grim said. The murder/suicide happened on a Saturday night after 11:00 p.m. As crowds poured through the neighborhood on their way home from a nearby Music Fest.

TEXAS /LUBY'S MASSACRE: On October 16, 1991, George Hennard deliberately drove his truck through the front window of a Luby's Cafeteria in Killeen, Texas, then opened fire on people inside. About 80 people were in the restaurant. He stalked, shot and murdered 23 people and wounded another 20 before committing suicide. During this rampage, he went up to Suzana Gratia Hupp and her parents. Hupp had in fact brought a handgun to the Luby's Cafeteria that day, but left it in her car due to the laws, restricting citizens at that time from carrying firearms.

According to her later testimony in favor of Missouri's HB—1720 bill and in general, after she realized that her firearm was not in her purse, but "a hundred feet away in her car," her father charged at Hennard to try and restrain him, but was shot to death. A short time later, her mother was also slain. Hupp later stated that she regretted obeying that gun law by leaving her weapon in her car, rather than keeping it on her person. One person inside Luby's broke a back window with a chair which gave others a way to escape. Hennard allowed a mother and her 4 year-old child to get out. He reloaded several times during the killings, committed suicide by shooting himself in the head after being cornered and wounded by police.

COLUMBINE: On Tuesday, April 20, 1999, the deadliest school shooting in United States history in a decade, occurred. Eleven students killed, 24 others wounded, before Eric Harris and Dillon Kleebold, students at Columbine High School committed suicide.

Ken Ham, Director, "Answers In Genesis": "We're reaping the consequences right now of the generation who have been taken through the publlic education school system and taught a Darwinian view toward that you can explain life by natural processes and therefore ultimately your morality is whatever you want it to be, and that's pretty much what is Darwinism.

Debbie Phillips niece, Rachael Scott, was one of the students killed at Columbine. "The killers, Eric and Dillon, badgered the kids repeatedly that day, taunting—"do you believe in God?"—then they murdered them when they refused to deny God.

While there were many factors that led to the Columbine shootings, the idea of Darwinian evolution, according to now deceased Dr. James Kennedy of Coral Ridge Ministries, played a part, "a significant role." Dr. Kennedy, on his report on the Columbine shootings said, "The autopsy report of Eric Harris revealed that on the day of the attack, he intentionally, the last day of his life, had chosen to wear a T-Shirt emblazoned with the words, "Natural Selection."

Denver area high school teacher, Dr. Ken Poppe, "To me, that was signifying that if natural selection is the person's point of view that is a fight for survival and the people who are the strongest are going to rule, and on that day I believe their armaments gave them the impression that they were the stronger and they had the right to deprive the lives of other students."

The killers had been planning the attack for almost a year. They picked April 20th to honor the birthday of one of their heroes, Adolph Hitler, who also was influenced by Darwinism.

They set bombs that never went off, but it failed. Their plan was to kill over 500 people that day.

Even though Columbine was a dramatic illustration of school shootings, there have been more than a dozen or more in the U.S. Since then.

Dr. James Kennedy, PhD., said that it's tragic, but, "Is it all that surprising? If you teach children that they're no more than trousered apes, and that life has no purpose or meaning, then why are we shocked when they act like that? Evolutionist George Demouira called man a fungus on the surface of one of the minor planets. Arnold Shoneburg referred to man as a hairless ape. As Supreme Court Justice Oliver Wendell Holmes said, 'I see no reason attributing to man a significant difference in kind to that which belongs to a grain of sand."

Dr. Kennedy continued, "Well, the fungus just got demoted. We wonder why our young people are killing themselves and others."

VIRGINIA TECH HIGH SCHOOL: On April 16, 2007, only four days before the 8th anniversary of the Columbine High School massacre where two students murdered 13 people, then committed suicide, a gunman at Virginia Tech High School shot to death two people in a dormitory before going next to classrooms on campus where he methodically murdered 10 more people before committing suicide.

In over a two and a half-hour period, at least 15 other people were wounded at Virginia Polytechnic Institute and State University. Some were injured when they jumped from windows to escape the killer.

When it was over students and staff demanded to know why the initial warning by police by e-mail, came two and a half hours late. Angry that the police delayed in responding for that long a period of time, even though the killer of two people was still at large. By then, he'd gone to classrooms and killed others. The total of murdered victims was 32, and another 15 were treated for gunshot wounds, and other injuries.

This high school massacre began around 7:15 a.m. At West Ambler Johnston, a co-educational residence hall that houses 895 people. The killer had a 9mlm. Pistol and a .22 caliber handgun and killed a man, and a woman at that Hall.

It wasn't until two and a half hours later that the police responded to the 911 call reporting that shots had been fired at Harris Hall, an engineering classroom building about a half-mile away on the opposite end of the 2,600 acre campus. They found that the front doors had been chained from the inside, apparently to keep police out, and students from escaping.

Police broke through the doors and followed the sound of gunshots to the 2nd floor, where they discovered the gunman who had shot himself in the face. As police searched the building, they found dozens of mortally wounded people, a total of 30 murdered by the gunman inside the building.

The killer was a senior English major at Virginia Tech. His name was Seung-Hui Cho, a South Korean who had moved to the United States when he was 8 years-old.

Cho had been diagnosed with a severe anxiety disorder that he had been getting treatment for since middle school. He had continued the therapy until his junior year of high school. While in college in 2005, Cho was accused of stalking two female students. At that time Cho was declared mentally ill by a Virginia Special Justice. One professor had encouraged Cho to get counseling.

Those murdered that day at Virginia Tech by Cho, were 5 faculty members, and 27 students, and many more wounded. While in an intermediate French language class in Norris Hall, Room 211, eleven students died. Nine students died in an advanced hydrology class in Room 206. Four students died in an elementary German language class in Room 207. One student died in a mechanics class in Room 204, Two students died at the West Ambler Johnston building earlier.

The Virginia Tech review panel reported that Cho's rampage wounded 17 other people, 6 more were injured when they jumped from 2nd story windows to escape.

Professor Liviu Librescu held the door of his classroom, Room 204, shut while, the killer tried to get in. Librescu was able to stop Cho until most of his students escaped through the windows, but died after Cho shot him multiple times through the door. One student also died in the classroom.

Jocelyne Couture-Nowak tried to save her students in the French classroom, Room 211, after facing Cho in the hallway. Colin Goddard, one of 7 survivors in the French class, told his family that Couture-Nowak ordered her students to the back of the class for their safety and made a fatal effort to block the door.

Student Henry Lee was also killed while trying to help Professor Couture-Nowak barricade the classroom door.

In Room 206, the stirring of a wounded Waleed Shaelam, distracted a student that was close by after Cho had returned to the room, where, a student eyewitness said that Shaalan was shot a second time and died.

Partahi Mamora Halomoan Lumbantoruan, also in Room 206, may have saved fellow student Guillermo Coleman by throwing his own body on top of him and taking multiple gunshots that killed him, but protected the other student.

Zach Petkewicz, a student, barricaded the door of Room 205 by moving a large table to the classroom door, after substitute professor Haiyan Cheng and an unidentified female student in the same class saw Cho walking toward them. Cho shot several times through the door but couldn't get in. Those inside were spared.

Kately Camey, Derek O'Dell Trey Perkins, and Erin Sheehar blocked the door of Room 207, the German class, after the first assault and helped the students who were wounded. Cho returned minutes later but O'Dell and Camey stopped him from getting back inside the classroom, but both were injured.

Professor Kevin Granata heard the gunfire and struggle on the floor below, and brought 20 students from a nearby classroom into an office, where the door could be locked, on the 3rd floor of Norris Hall. The professor then went downstairs to investigate and was shot and killed by Cho. All of the students, Professor Granata had locked in his office were not injured.

Virginia Tech students afterwards expressed their belief that many could have been saved that day if campus officials had taken immediate action to secure the campus after the first assault by Cho at the dormitory. "I really thought they should have canceled classes sooner," Sam Leake, a junior who lives in West Ambler Johnston, said to the college paper, The Collegiate Times. "If they had, maybe some of these deaths would have been prevented."

"At first I thought it was a joke," another student said who was shot in the arm. "You don't really think of a gunman coming on campus and shooting people."

TOWER SNIPER, AUSTIN, TEXAS; Charles Whitman was a student at the University of Texas who shot and killed 14 people and wounded 31 others from the observation deck of the University's Main Building of the University of Texas at Austin on August 11, 1966. Whitman committed these murders after killing his wife and his mother. He was killed by Austin Police.

The first shots from the tower's outer deck came at approximately 11:48 a.m. A history professor was the first one to call Austin Police Department after seeing several students shot in the South Mall gathering center, many others had dismissed the rifle shots, not realizing it was gunfire. Eventjually the gunfire created panic as news spread and it was clear what was happening and all police were ordered to the campus. Other off-duty officers, sheriff's deputies, and Texas department of Public Safety officers also were called upon and assisted.

As soon as Whitman started getting return gunfire, he used the waterspouts on each side of the tower as gun ports, which allowed him to continue shooting, being protected from the return fire by law enforcement below. Also joining the police were civilians who brought guns to assist police. Ramiro Martinez, an officer credited with subduing Whitman's threat, later stated in his book that the civilians assisting should be credited as they made it difficult for Whitman to take careful aim without being hit. Police lieutenant and sharpshooter, Marion Lee reported from a small airplane that there was only one sniper firing from the parapet. The plane circled the tower trying to get a shot at Whitman, but the turbulence shook the plane too badly for him to get Whitman in his sights.

As the airplane was being fired on, Lee asked the pilot to back off but to stay close enough to offer him a target and keep him worried. The plane, which was hit approximately 13 times, stayed with it until Whitman was killed.

Whitman fired indiscriminately and most of the victims were shot on Guadeloupe Street, a major commercial and business district across the west side of the campus.

Police officer Ramiro Martinez and Houston McCoy, Jerry Day, quickly deputized citizen Allen Crum, and went up towards the observation deck. Martinez and McCoy, armed with a .38 revolver and a shotgun, stepped out on the observation deck, proceeded to the northeast corner of the deck, and spotted Whitman seated on the floor watching the southwest corner for any police.

McCoy fired his shotgun twice, and Martinez fired six rounds from his revolver before taking the shotgun and approaching the unmoving Whitman and firing again point-blank. They then took the green towel that Whitman had brought with him, and waved it to those below, a signal that the sniper had been taken out.

Following the Tower Shooting, the observation deck was closed for 2 years, and opened again in 1968. However, after several suicides, it was re-closed in 1974 and remained closed until September 15, 1999. Under supervised security measures, the observation deck can now be visited through guided tours only. Still visible on the limestone walls are bullet scars.

BATH SCHOOL DISASTER; According to police reports and local Bath, Michigan newspapers, May 19, 1927, "maniac blows-up school, kills 42, mostly children. He had "protested high taxes," was reportedly the motivation for the massacre. Of the victims, 33 were pupils. He then kills himself and 3 others by dynamiting his automobile."

The report continued that the insane revenge of a man maddened by financial worries brought death to at least 33 children when the Consolidated School in the little village of "300 souls" was dynamited just after the morning bell had called the classes together.

The north end of the school collapsed, and "undoubtedly bodies are buried in the debris." Eighty-five to 95 were injured.

Andrew Kehoe, Treasurer of the village School Board, was the man who placed in the basement of the school the dynamite that wrecked one wing of the building and brought death and injury to children and teachers. Kehoe's house and barn, a mile or so out of town, were destroyed in another explosion and fire caused by himself a little before the blast in the school.

Kehoe himself was killed, together with Emory E. Huyck, Superintendent of the school. Kehoe's remains were put in unknown grave with no marker. At the order of coroner C.E. Lamb what remained of Andrew Kehoe's body was brought to St. Johns late Wednesday, May 18, 1927. The next afternoon, a sister, Miss Agnes Kehoe of Battle Creek, claimed the body and made arrangements for the burial.

On Friday afternoon, unknown to the public, the remains were taken to Mt. Rest Cemetery and placed in a grave. There was no minister, no friends, no relatives, not even an undertaker present. There was no marker placed on the grave.

A mortgage on Kehoe's farm was foreclosed a week before. He had complained that the high school taxes made it impossible for him to lift the mortgage. It was believed that Kehoe's act of insanity was caused by his desire for revenge on the School Board. One teacher was killed and 3 were seriously injured. The village postmaster was injured and later died.

Under the lurid glare of searchlights playing on a tangled bed of ruins, State Police and volunteer workers searched the rubble for missing children. The list of dead was placed at 42.

The explosion in the school came at 9:40 a.m., ten minutes after classes began. About 260 pupils were in the building. The entire north wing of the building was shattered, which housed the 3rd, 4th, 5th, and 6th grades.

Children in the South Wing were uninjured. Most of the children in the unshattered position of the building were led to safety by the teachers.

State Police, exploring the basement of that part of the building found it undamaged by the explosion. The police discovered about 500 pounds of dynamite planted in such a manner that a portion was under every room in the school. If it had exploded, the school would have been demolished and almost every child would have been killed.

FINLAND SCHOOL SHOOTING: Finnish police looked through web-sites for links between the teenager who plotted a Columbine-like assault in Montgomery County and Pekka-Eric Auyinen. The teenagers had communicated by e-mail, apparently out of a common interest in the Columbine school shootings and violent video games

Plymouth Meeting resident, Dillon Cossay, 14, had been trading e-mail with the Finland "recognized the screen name and recalled having contact," said J. David Farell, who represents Cossey. Montgomery County D.A. Bruce L. Castor, Jr., took a second look at material on Cossey's computer. Cossay told Farrell that in the e-mails, Auvienen, "gave no indication he was going to do anything violent," and that Cossay "offered nothing in the way of encouragement." He learned of the incident from his attorney.

Police seized the computer, along with a 9 mlm. Semi-automatic carbine, knives, and hand grenades, BB guns, swords, violent videos, anad a bomb-making manual. Cossay admitted to his plans to attack Plymouth Whitemarsh High School. His treatment program will last until he is 21.

In Tuusula, Finland on November 08, 2007, an 18 year-old gunman who killed seven other students and the principal before killing himself in a rampage, was a "social outcast who was bullied in school," a senior police official stated to World News.

Investigation said the gunman, Pekka-Eric Auvinen, shot himself in the head after the shooting spree at Jokela High School in Tuusula, some 30 miles north of the capital, Helsinki.

Finnish Prime Minister Matti Van Hauten described the bloodshed as "extremely tragic," and declared a day of National mourning with flags to be flown half-staff. Grieving students placed candles outside the school.

The teen killed five boys, two girls and the female principal with a .22 caliber pistol. Officials said one person was wounded by a bullet and about a dozen others suffered other injuries while fleeing the killer.

Witnesses described a scene of mayhem at the school at this leafy, lakeside community, saying the gunman prowled the school looking for victims while shouting slogans for "revolution."

Police Chief Mattie Tohkanen, said the gunman didn't have a previous criminal record, "he was from an ordinary family. He had belonged to a gun club and had obtained a license for a pistol.

The residents in Tuusula, a town of 34,000, said that such assaults were unheard of in the area. "Mostly nothing happens here, these are nice surroundings, and not any criminals to talk of. This was a total surprise," were the comments of Reijo Pekka, whose son Arttu Sittala was at the school.

"When we heard the shots we started breaking the windows and jumping," a 14 year-old student, Fraunz Andersen, said. Another student, Miro Luknmaa, said to the local paper, Iltalehti, "I saw injured people lying in the corridor. We started to run and followed the crowd in panic. Everyone was trying to squeeze through a narrow door."

JONESTOWN MASSACRE: The first reports out of Guyana on November 18, 1978 were that congressman Leo J. Ryan and four other members of his party were shot and killed as they attempted to board a plane at Port Kaituma airstrip.

Within hours, came the shocking announcement that 408 American citizens had committed suicide at a communal village they had built in the jungle in Northwest Guyana.

The dead were all members of a group known as "The People's Temple," which was led by the Reverend Jim Jones. It would soon be learned that 913 of the 1,100 people believed to have been at "Jonestown" at the time, had died in a mass suicide.

Based on the official report submitted to U.S. House of Representaatives on May 15, 1979, the chain of events leading to Leo Ryan's death in Guyana began a year earlier, after he read an article entitled, "Scared Too Long," related the death of Sam Houston's son, Bob, in October 1976. Houston had decided to speak out about his son's death because he believed that the reason Bob had died, beneath the wheels of a train, was because he had announced his decision to leave the People's Temple the day before.

Houston was also concerned that his two grand daughters, sent to New York for vacation, had ended up in "Jonestown," village. There were claims of social security irregularities, human rights violations and that people were being held against their will at "Jonestown." In June of 1978, Ryan read excerpts from the sworn affidavit of Debbie Blakely, a defector from "Jonestown," which included claims that the community at "Jonestown" had on a number of occasions, rehearsed for a mass suicide. After meeting with a number of concerned relatives, Ryan's interesst in the People's Temple became widely known and the reports about the group both favorable and unfavorable, began to pour in. He hired an attorney to interview former People's Temple members and relatives of members to determine whether there had been any violation of Federal and State laws by the group.

In September, 1978, Ryan met with Vernon P. Vaky and other State Department officials to discuss the possibility of Ryan making a trip to "Jonestown" in Guyana. Permission was granted and the trip was planned for the week of November 12-18. Ryan's intention to visit "Jonestown" soon became widely known and the numbers wishing to accompany him had grown substantially by the time of his departure. There were 9 extra media people and 18 representatives from a delegation of Concerned Relatives who would go with him, at their own expense. The official party, or Codel, consisted of Ryan, James Schollaert, and Jackie Speier, Ryan's personal assistant.

Problems began for the group as soon as they arrived in Guyana; from the San Francisco Chronicle. Ryan was detained overnight at the airport, as he did not have an entry visa. The group of Concerned Relatives, despite having confirmed reservations, had to spend the night in the lobby of the Pegasus Hotel in Georgetown because there were no rooms available to them. Over the next two and a half days, Ryan met with Embassy personnel and organized a meeting with Ambassador Burke and the Concerned Relatives. He and the relatives attempted to speak with a representative of the People's Temple at their headquarters in Georgetown, but could not gain entry. In addition, Ryan was not able to negotiate successfully with Lane or Garry, another legal representative of the People's Temple, resulting in the postponement of the scheduled flight to the mission until Friday, November 17th.

The negotiation still had made no headway on Friday morning so Ryan informed Lane and Garry that he and that he and his party would be leaving for "Jonestown" at 2:30 pm. There were two seats on the plane if Lane and Garry wished to leave with them. The plane left as scheduled.

Upon their arrival at "Jonestown," the delegation was served dinner and entertained. As the evening progressed, reporters interviewed Jim Jones while Ryan and Speier talked to the People's Temple members where names had been provided by relatives in the U.S. During he course of the evening, a "Jonestown" member passed a note to NBC reporter Dean Harris indicating that he and his family wished to leave. Another member made a similar request to Dwyer. Both requests were reported to Ryan.

At 11:00 pm, the media and family representatives were returned to Port Kaituma as Jim Jones refused to allow them to spend the night on the compound. Ryan, Speier, Dwyer, Amibourne, Lane and Garry were the only ones who spent the night of Friday, the 17th of November at "Jonestown."

At Port Kaituma, local Guyana, including one police official who told stories of alleged beatings at "Jonestown," approached media representatives. They complained that Guyana officials were denied entry to the compound and had no authority there. They also described a "torture hole" in the compound.

Media and relatives were not returned to "Jonestown" until 11:00 am the next day, several hours later than planned. Ryan had continued interviewing members since early in the morning, during which time other member individuals told of their desire to leave. By 3:00 pm there were a total of 15 People's Temple members climbing into the trucks with the delegation to drive to Port Kaituma airport. Ryan had intended to stay, but was attacked by People's Temple member Don Sly, with a knife. He was not hurt, but Dwyer insisted that Ryan leave with them. Dwyer planned to return to "Jonestown" later to resolve a dispute with a family member who was split on the question of leaving "Jonestown."

The party arrived at Port Kaituma airport at about 4:30 pm. The delay had been caused by the unexpected request to the U.S. Embassy for a second plane to carry the extra 15 passengers.

Soon after its arrival, a six—passenger Cessna was loaded and ready to leave. As it began to taxi to the far end of the airstrip, one of the "Jonestown" defectors on board, Larry Layton, opened fire on the other passengers.

At the same time, as Ryan's party were boarding the other plane, a twin-engine Otter, occupants of a tractor and trailer owned by the People's Temple, opened fire. Ryan, and three members of the media and one of the defectors were killed.

Speir and five others were seriously wounded. The shooting lasted between 4 to 5 minutes and the larger plane was disabled. The Cessna was able to take off and reported news of the attack to controllers at the Georgetown tower. They in turn notified the Guyana officials. The attack left the airport soon after, while survivors of the attack sought cover and protection for the night.

According to the official report, the mass suicide began at about 5:00 pm At about 6:00 p.m., Ambassador Burke was informed of the shooting. He, in turn, informed the U.S. State Department at 8:30 pm by cable. At approximately 7:00 pm, Guyaba Oikuce told Sherwin Harris, a member of the Concerned Relatives group, that his ex-wife, Sharon Amos, and three of her children were found dead at the People's Temple headquarters in Georgetown.

Word of the deaths at "Jonestown" reached Port Kaituma on Sunday morning when survivors, Stanley Clayton and Odell Rhodes arrived there.

At dawn, Sunday, the 19th of November, the first contingent of Guyana Army rescue forces arrived in Port Kaituma. More soldiers arrived within the hour. All of the wounded and most of the survivors were airlifted from Port Kaituma before nightfall and transferred to U.S. Air force medical evacuation aircraft in Georgetown.

The moments before the mass suicide at "Jonestown," the final decision to die brought resistance from a few, but armed guards who surrounded the room shot many of them. Of the estimated 1,100 people believed to have been present at "Jonestown" at the time, 913 died, including Jim Jones. The rest somehow escaped into the jungle.

SUICIDE BOMBERS: I only include this sub-set of humans and suicide as my definition of a suicide-bomber, perceived by me, to be an extinction of self to become a martyr to serve hatred—not God. A "good" example of a rage of vanities akin to Lucifer, and that sin-entity's dark fall from grace.

Chapter Eight

Jumping To A Conclusion

A "jumper" is someone who commits suicide by jumping to a conclusion of their life from a bridge or tower or building or any significant height. Images come to mind of a person sitting on a ledge of a building several to many stories high. Or they're standing, a little off balance, while police are shouting through bullhorns trying to talk the distraught person down.

CASE ONE: October 13, 2003

On the morning of March 19, a man took a walk across the Golden Gate Bridge. He intended to kill himself. He climbed the four-foot safety railing and lowered himself onto the bridge's outermost 32" wide beam, called "the chord," 220 feet above the San Francisco Bay.

Survivors often regret their decision in mid-air. Ken Baldwin and Kevin Hines both say they hurdled over the railing, afraid that if they stood on the chord they might lose their courage. Baldwin was 28 and severely depressed that day in August, 1985, when he told his wife not to expect him home until late. "I wanted to disappear," he said. "So, the Golden Gate Bridge was the spot. I'd heard that the water just sweeps you under." On the bridge, Baldwin counted to ten and stayed frozen. He counted to ten again, then jumped. "I still see my hands coming off the railing," he said, as he crossed the chord in flight, Baldwin recalls, "I instantly realized that everything in my life that I'd thought was unfixable was totally fixable—except for having just jumped."

Kevin Hines was 18 years-old when he took a bus to the Golden Gate Bridge one day in September, 2000. He dove into hes "last meal" of Star

Bursts and Skittles while pacing back and forth for at least half an hour, crying and distraught. No one, he recalled, asked him if he needed help, and a tourist from Germany asked him if he would take her picture. His thoughts, he said, were, "f—this. Nobody cares," and jumped. My first thought was what the hell did I just do? I don't want to die."

At a rally (1977) on the Golden Gate Bridge supporting the building of an anti-suicide barrier above the railing, a minister tried to explain the allure for jumpers. "The bridge is a symbol," he said, "that presides over the end of the continent, and just being there left him in a rather suicidal mood. The Golden Gate is a symbol of human integrity, technological genius, but social failure."

Every two or three weeks, someone jumps off the Golden Gate Bridge. It's the one spot suicidal people go in the world who intend to jump to their conclusion. Since the opening of the bridge, over twelve hundred people committed suicide by jumping from the bridge. Some wrap suicide notes in plastic and put it in a pocket.

The Golden Gate has a footpath adjacent to a low, exterior railing. "Jumping from the bridge is seen as sure, quick and clean and available—which is the most potent factor," said Dr. Jerome Motto, a local psychiatrist and suicide expert in San Francisco.

Over ten million tourists travel to see the spectacular but notorious bridge annually.

'It's a four-second fall from the bridge, and said to herself on the way down, "I must be about to hit," over and over in her mind.'

They are wrong to think it's "a clean hit." Coroner reports tell of suicides caused by "multiple-blunt-force-injuries." Jumpers who hit the water are impacting at around 75 mph, with a force of 15,000 lbs per square inch. Eighty-five per-cent suffer broken ribs, which rip inward to tear the spleen, the lungs, and the heart. And the vertebrae snap, and the liver ruptures.

The famous bridge in San Francisco is noted for its beauty, its unique form and architecture, and the panoramic ocean scape of the Pacific Coast. Some jump from the Golden Gate Bridge under the illusion that they will experience a kind of grace—a welcoming body of water that inducts the jumper into nature. The coroner's previous statement about what in reality happens to the body obliterates that notion.

One jumper recalls, "I'd heard the water just sweeps you under." Understanding the coroner's report, there is nothing serene or peaceful about exploding body parts on impact at 75mph and a force of 15,000 lbs per square inch. The jumper dies instantly from extreme internal injuries; others drown in their own blood.

The Psychiatric Foundation of Northern California did a study for the Marin County coroner's office. In that study, three to one were men, 87 per-cent are Bay area residents; they range from 14-85, with an approximate median age of 41. Some leave suicide notes, but most don't. An estimated 26 jumpers have survived.

The first jumper, on August 07, 1937, was Harold Wolder, a World War I veteran. Wolder turned to a stranger on the walkway, and said, "This is as far as I go," and jumped.

Robert Blyther was a 27 year-old Navy Veteran, flew from Virginia to San Francisco in December, 1980 to jump off the bridge. His motivation? To protest the election of Ronald Reagan as president.

Filomena De La Cruz, celebrated Thanksgiving with relatives in 1993, then took his two year-old son along the bridge. At about 5:00 in the evening, De La Cruz lifted his child out of the stroller, grasped him in his arms and jumped over the guardrail. "He was going through a divorce and custody fight," a homicide inspector said at the time.

Weldon Kees, 40, was a poet and a film maker who produced KPFA's radio show, "Behind the Movie Camera." Kees parked his 1954 Plymouth Savoy at the bridge parking lot on July 1955 and left his keys in the ignition and disappeared. His body was never found.

In 2004, Jonathan Zablotny, a senior at International High School, became a "jumping statistic". "Overall, he had more reason to be happy than to kill himself," a friend said. In a letter to the bridge district board, Patrick Fitzgerald wrote, "He told no one and left no note. All we know is that he left for school Tuesday morning and never got there. That afternoon he was dead."

There are other suicide targets, like the Eiffel tower and the Empire State Building where officials have put up safety barriers. People in San Francisco say quiet about their bridge being a "death magnet." They don't want to discuss suicide in their city which describes attitude of, "They'll jump someplace else if they didn't do it here, anyway."

TOKYO VOLCANO:

In January, 1933, two classmates from a Tokyo school jumped into Mount Mihara, an active volcano on the Japanese Island of Oshima. Weeks later six more jumped into the volcano. Soon tourists were gathering to witness the suicides which totaled 140 that year, 160 the next. Barriers were erected and today it's not considered as a suicide destination.

In 1974, sociologist David Phillips gave a different name to suicide copycats. He called it the "Werther effect," taking the name from, "The Sorrows of Young Werther," an 18th century German novel by Johann Wolfgang von Goethe. The story of a young man's suicide by pistol after a failed romance, "Sorrows", inspired a rash of follow-suit-suicides—many of whom dressed for death in the style of the novel's hero—until the book was banned in several countries.

The newspaper accounts are thought to have been behind "the Werther effect," which is reportedly the reason why The Centers for Disease Control and Prevention and the American Association of Suicidology issues guidelines urging the newspapers and media to downplay the suicides at the Golden Gate Bridge, especially since in the '90's, a suicide club was formed to predict he exact date that the 1,000[th] suicide would jump to their death.

TWO OPPOSITE VIEWS OF "THE JUMP":

First Quote: "When someone jumps from that bridge (GGB) he is in a way, joining all those who went before. And that's important, I believe, because even in suicide, people don't like to be too far removed from the herd." East Bay psychiatrist Malcomb A. Sower

Second Quote: "Most of the people who are suicidal are so wound up in themselves, so depressed and so unable to see beyond the tip of their nose that the idea of becoming part of the larger congregation wouldn't really appeal to them. They're really stuck in one place, sort of glued into the fact that there's no hope for them, no future, no alternatives. They get a kind of tunnel vision," Dr. Seiden of U.C. Berkeley.

EIFFEL TOWER;

There have been over 400 suicide jumpers from the Eiffel Tower. In ninety years there have been only two who survived. They survived the 57 meter drop from the first floor, one being blown onto a rafter by the wind and the other landing on the roof of a car. The latter was a young woman who after recovering married the owner of the car she landed.

CHINA:

In Nanjung, China at the Yangtze River Bridge, a Mr. Chen notices a man standing alone, seemingly deep in thought, and walked toward him. He watched people getting off city buses and took measure of the slump of their shoulders as they trudged along the sidewalk at the edge of the bridge.

Mr. Chen watched and waited for that moment in time when the unthinkable act would appear on his bridge and someone would try to jump off. Mr. Chen comes almost every week-end, bringing a thermos of tea. He has become the bridge's self-appointed guardian angel. "If I save one person," Mr. Chen said, "One is a lot." This guardian angel believes he has prevented at least 42 people from jumping since he began his patrol a year ago. Mr. Chen, in his mid-30's has talked them down and wrestled with them. He has also watched five people slip out of his grasp and fall to their deaths in the Yangtze.

Mr. Chen took on the job of watching for signs of trouble in people's soul's. He watched people, especially the lone figures staring down at the water.

"It's very easy to recognize," he said of likely jumpers. "A person walks without spirit."

Mr. Chen said he comes to the bridge because someone needs to. Suicide is presently the leading cause of death for Chinese aged 15-34. The Yangtze River Bridge, like major bridges in other countries, attracts a continual crowd of jumpers. At least 1,000 people are believed to have jumped since its opening in 1968.

"The fact that he's doing this as a volunteer is very helpful," said Dr. Michael Phillips, the executive director of the Beijing Suicide Research and Prevention Center. A decade ago, Dr. Phillips said, the police might have arrested Mr. Chen, but now the government is allowing a little more space for some forms of activism. The officers on the bridge know him by name. One of the officers said they regularly stop jumpers but that the main section of the bridge, nearly a mile in length, is too long to protect everyone. Mr. Chen said some people come by taxi, stop in the middle of the span, pay their fare, then get out and climb over the railing.

"We have to teach people to love life and treasure life," said Mr. Chen, who makes a living selling small commercial billboards.

PHILIPPINES:

A garbage scavenger in the Philippines threatened to jump from the 3rd floor of the Metro Rail Transit in Manila.

Herman Okkoseba sat on the edge of a concrete platform with his feet dangling as cars passed beneath him. Witnesses reported that the man looked like he was about to jump from the 50-foot high building.

A parking attendant at a fast food chain near the MRT station called police. A rescue team from the National Capitol Region Police Office special Action force, went to the 3rd floor to intervene. Agents of the SAF looped a nylonn cord around Okoseba from behind and rescued him.

At that time, he said he'd wanted to end his life because he couldn't find a job. He believed it was because he was lame, and people didn't want to hire him. MRT officials and police took him to a hospital to get psychiatric treatment.

PENNSYLVANIA:

"Nine stories. It's amazing that I'm still alive," said Jordan Burnham, 18 years-old and a senior at Upper Merion High School outside Philadelphia. Jordan was a popular student and athlete who had been chosen for homecoming court two years in a row. But, he was overcome with depression, despite medication and treatment for it.

On September 28, 2008, he jumped from the nine story apartment in King of Prussia, hit the ground at 50mph, landing on his left side and breaking his pelvis. His left leg was shattered above and below the knee. His left wrist, skull and jaw were fractured and extensive internal bleeding.

Trauma surgeon Patrick Reilly, who treated Burnham, said that he survived the fall because he land3d on earth instead of asphalt, and because he didn't land on his head or neck. He was also young and fit and received immediate medical attention.

"The fact that he fell nine stories certainly puts his survival as sort of an exceptional event," added Dr. Reilly. "Someone who falls nine stories, the majority of those patients would die, many before they ever reach medical attention."

THE 1929 STOCK MARKET CRASH:

When the great crash of 1929 happened, reporters gathered in Manhattan to check out a rumor that eleven bankrupt investors had plunged out of windows to their death. Will Rogers remarked, "When Wall Street took that tail spin, you had to stand in line to get a window to jump out of, and speculators were selling space for bodies in the east river."

Although the U.S. Suicide rate increased between 1925 and 1932, economist John Kenneth Galbraith studied the death certificates during October and November of 1929 and found that suicides were not reported in great numbers.

The president of the County Trust company on Friday, November 5, 1929, J.J. Riordan took a gun from a teller's cage at his bank, went to his home in downtown Manhattan and shot himself. The news of this, however, was not announced until after the bank closed at noon Saturday to prevent causing a run on the bank.

A vice-president of the Earl Radio Corporation jumped to his death from a window of a Manhattan Hotel. He left this suicide note: "We are broke. Last April, I was worth 100,000. Today, I am $24,000 in the red." But he jumped weeks before the crash.

Winston Churchill was visiting New York during that time. On the following day after Black Tuesday, he was awakened by the noise of a crowd outside the Savoy-Plaza Hotel. "Under my very window, a gentleman cast himself down fifteen stories and was dashed to pieces, causing a wild commotion and the arrival of the fire brigade," Churchill wrote.

At New York's empire State Building, a lawyer jumped to his death from his 69th floor office. In the fall, it severed a leg that crashed to the sidewalk in front of horrified onlookers. Severed below the knee, it was bare, except for a gray and black sock. Police said that the rest of his body was discovered intact on a 30th floor landing.

The jumper was identified as Moshe Kanawsky, 31 years-old. There was no clear reason for the suicide." He was interviewing a client," said a man who worked in the same suite. "He just got up, opened the window and jumped."

Since the Empire State Building opened in 1931, at least 30 people have jumped to their death. David Abramowitz died when he jumped from the 66th floor on February 02, 2006, after buying a ticket to the 86th floor observation deck.

A depressed rabbi and a part-time lawyer, David Kavnosky, jumped from an office building in Maryland where he worked. "It's not something anybody should have to deal with," his father said. "Not because of the pain I feel, but because of he loss of such a promising 31 year-old man not being able to make a significant impact on the world."

After graduating from Yeshiva Ner Israel, in Baltimore, Kavnosky went to Israel where he studied at one of the top schools in the country. Shortly after he returned to Maryland to enroll at the Ner Israel Rabbinical College, family said that he had begun to shows signs of depression. His friends also said that he became more and more withdrawn and would sleep for hours in the middle of the day.

His financial problems were serious and couldn't see the best doctors because he wasn't able to afford it. Because of his finances, a friend said, "he ended up seeing a multitude of psychiatrists."

THE AURORA BRIDGE:

Located in Seattle, the first jumper was a shoe salesman, who leaped to his death from the bridge in January, 1932, a month before it officially opened. Since then, more than 200 people have jumped from the Aurora Bridge, including a former council member

Media coverage from the '70 marked Aurora Seattle's "suicide bridge" after 9 people jumped in 1972, the worst year of jumper suicides on record. On average, four people a year die.

Research indicates that people who choose to jump to commit suicide, do so believing that the plunge will create the velocity they think is necessary to finish off their misery. The free fall accelerates to about 55mph in four seconds.

Social Service Agencies and university researchers have studied bridge jumpers in nearly every industrialized country. From Stockholm to Istanbul to Seattle, the similarities are significant. The majority are men between 35 and 40 years-old, and most have some form of mental problem. And most didn't leave a suicide note.

A woman who works near the Aurora Bridge parking lot, said, "Newspapers don't usually report suicide, so it kind of happens in a vacuum." She recalled what one of her co-workers had said. One morning he saw something in the parking lot and walked toward it. At first he thought it was junk, then a pile of carpet, then when he got closer, a dog. Only when he walked right up did he see a face.

These people who work close by, see it about four times a year. When they pull in to the parking lot, a portion of it is roped off with yellow tape, emergency trucks and personnel. They develop a personal, yet detached attitude about suicide.

Some bodies hit the water, but many don't. They hit the Adobe parking lot or in neighborhoods. A crew team witnessed a jump just 50 feet away, and another jumper's body hit a vehicle while the driver was still in it.

Parking lots have been painted to remove blood stains. One man moved his small business away from inside a houseboat under the bridge after seeing the outcome of these suicides too many times.

NEW YORK AREA

Port Authorities of New York and New Jersey reported that a man just released from a hospital after an attempted suicide jump, went right back to another bridge and tried it again. The homeless man, Jose Bicet, was talked down from the overpass by rescue workers. The first jump was off an overpass above Route 495, and his rescuer that time was Mayor Bruce Walter of Union City.

In Greenwich, Connecticut, a young woman who was not identified, jumped off the Tappan Zee Bridge in September, 1996, after her van hit a guardrail. A New York State Thruway Authority, John Cardilo, said that after she jumped into the Hudson River, a volunteer firefighter jumped right after her and saved her. Witnesses said Daniel Santos, the firefighter, seemed to have been knocked unconscious when he hit the water, but quickly regained consciousness and began to swim toward the woman, who was floating not far from him. A boat was sent by the Tarrytown Yacht Club to help in the rescue, and pulled them both from the water.

"We were at the bottom of the Brooklyn Bridge when the call came in," said Officer Richard Hare. An unidentified woman had climbed over the edge of the Manhattan Bridge. "We drove out and saw a group of pedestrians and bicyclist on the walkway who were waving us down and pointing. We couldn't even see her without looking over the side. When I looked over, my heart just dropped. She was right on the edge, about five feet below the roadway, sitting on a girder about a foot and a half wide. She was facing forward with nothing in front of her except air and water," said Officer Hare

"We were hanging off the bridge," Officer Hare continued. "Between my knees and my thighs there is a dirt mark about a foot wide from the girder. I could have just touched her and she would jump. I was saying the basic things, "Come on, life's not that bad. If you want to see your children, I'll take you to them."

As the officers were talking with her, she would inch closer to the edge every few minutes, and made a lunge over the side s a special rescue unit came close. Officer Hare grabbed for her, and another officer, Mark Brager, held onto her under her right arm. While the two officers held onto her, the four special unit Emergency Medical Service workers clung onto the police officers, legs and belts as they hung upside down.

"Her whole body was over the water," Officer Hare said. "She was dangling over the side like a shirt on a clothesline flopping in the wind. We could hear her shirt starting to tear. There was a small orange Coast Guard boat down below waiting to catch her. We couldn't have lifted ourselves up; that was impossible. As they lifted up, she was kicking and fighting. She was screaming, 'let go!' and we just kept hanging on for dear life." Officer Hare concluded his account.

Bridge jumpers, like the ones at the Golden Gate Bridge in San Francisco, believe that jumping is the way to go because it's quick oblivion as the water sweeps you under. But, they couldn't be more wrong. Death by jumping to a conclusion, is painful and grotesque, with them drowning in their own blood of a crushed organ or severed limb when they hit the water, only their screams drowned out by the water.

OBIT/ "AN EXTREME SPORTS-RISK-TAKER CHOSE TO CLIMB
MT. EVEREST DESPITE BAD WEATHER REPORTS AND
NO GUIDE, FELL TO HIS DEATH TODAY..."

Chapter Nine

Edge Walkers At Risk—Or Suicidal Intent?

Suicide and extreme sports? The sports arena is being looked into because of the events of psychiatric problems and the real danger of athletes committing suicide. Reviewers from International Sports Medicine are researching athletes who have suicidal thoughts, attempted or completed suicide.

"I constantly have death in the back of my mind," said an extreme skier. It is believed by some experts that those enthusiasts who are so inclined to risk life and limb, don't have adequate information—psychologically and environmentally—before assuming the risk But, on the other hand, there are experts that believe that the high-stakes-risk-takers are the types thaat founded America.

And risky sports has become so big that it isn't risky business! At the top of the game in risky, extreme sports is mountain climbing. Derek Hersey, 36, was well acquainted with living on the edge. Not like other rock climbers, Derek climbed "free solo"—alone and using nothing but climbing shoes, finger chalk and quick-witted skills. A friend said, "Hersey went for the adrenaline and risk." In May of 1993, Derek was high on the face of Yosemite's Sentinel Rock when it began to rain. His friends found his battered body, and surmised that the over 300 feet fall was caused by slippery rocks.

Psychologists in the past might have written Derek off as a "sports nut" who fulfills a death-wish. Today's theorists are of the opinion that the average person prefers certainty.

It would appear, however, that researchers are finding out that it may not be a "death wish" after all. Studies are now inclined to believe that high risk takers are hard-wired-in-the-brain that is linked to pleasure centers and thrill-seeking. In addition to that, it functions like an addiction, affects maybe one in five people, and decreases with age.

Researchers aren't exactly sure how the risk-urge originates or what role the culture, heredity and environment play. And while it is understood that everyone has risk-taking behavior on some levels, like riding in a car, or crossing a street or eating at any fast-food place or restaurant these days.

There is a positive, upside to risk taking, of course. To take chances takes courage and faith. Some scientists, Frank Farley, PhD, for example, firmly believe that the willingness to take on a high risk challenge is necessary for success. The inner strength that drove Derek Hersey to rock climb, is the same drive another person harnesses to "run for office," said Dr. Farley.

There's another side to this—a darker side of risk taking. High risk takers, according to researchers, are "easily bored." They may also be bored with their jobs and lives in general. A desire for stimulation can make them more likely to seek danger, bet on the horses or go outside legal and moral boundaries. People who don't have a purpose and a meaning in their lives that God wants us to have is a likely candidate for extreme sports.

NIAGARA FALLS IN A BARREL:

> On October 24, 1901, Annie Taylor was the first person to go over Niagara Falls in a barrel. After she climbed inside her airtight wooden barrel, the air pressure was compressed to a 30 psi with a bicycle pump.
> July 25, 1911: The infamous Bobby Leuch plunged over the Falls in a steel barrel. Bobby broke both his kneecaps and his jaw during this daredevil stunt. Years later while touring in New Zealand, Bobby slipped on an orange peel and died from complications due to gangrene.
> July 11, 1920: Englishman Charles G. Stevens equipped his wooden barrel with an anvil for ballast. Charles tied himself to the anvil for security, after the plunge, Chuck's right arm was the only thing left in the barrel.
> July 24, 1928: "Smiling Jean" Lussier survived the ride over the brink in a large rubber ball.

> July 5, 1930: A Greek waiter named George L. Statakia suffocated to death after his barrel was trapped behind the Falls for more than 14 hours.
> June 30, 1961: Nathan Boya dropped off the brink in a ball-like contraption.
> July 03, 1984: The first Canadian to conquer the Falls was Karel Soucek. Karel survived the plunge, but later that year, he was killed while recreating the drop from a platform inside the Houston Astrodome. (Karel's barrel hit the edge of the water tank)
> October 01, 1995: Robert Overcraer, rode a jetski over the edge of the Horseshoe Falls to help promote awareness for the homeless. His parachute didn't open and Robert ended up promoting better parachutes.

BULL RIDING:

Cowboys know the risks, still they get on board. Joshua "Cody" Brenner, 21, knew the risks, but the thrill of riding a 2,000 lb. dynamo of rage was his dream, "a destiny," said a friend.

Brenner died at a Topeka, Kansas hospital after the bull he was riding at the Kansas Expo Center stepped on his abdomen. A friend who traveled with him on the rodeo circuit said everyone knew the dangers as they strap themselves to the bucking beasts. "But when you jump off after a successful ride, throw your hat off and hear the crowd cheer, there's nothing better in the whole world," said his friend, Steve Tracy. He remembers seeing his friend come out of the chute that Saturday night and hang-on for the full eight seconds before letting go. Something went wrong in the dismount and then a hoof caught Brenner in the torso and he didn't get back up.

Based on a study in the June issue of the International sports Med Journal, bull riders receive more injury than players in any other spectator sport Those injuries are often more serious, too, the study showed. Even so, those cowboys still live up to ride a raging bull.

Bull riding had its start in the Old West by rough-hewn American settlers. That pioneering, rough and ready spirit is still going strong in the modern day cowboy rodeo.

There are deaths in bull riding. Dr. Mark Brandenburg is with the University of Oklahoma College of Medicine and the organizer of the

International Rodeo Medicine Conference didn't have statistics on deaths related to rodeo events, but varying rodeo organizations estimated one to two people die each year just from the bull riding events.

"A lot of people do think it's crazy," Steve Tracey remarked, "Joshua Brenner wore protective gear, even a helmet," said URA president Clint Tatum. "It just shows even when everything goes right, it's still possible to get hurt."

In every rodeo there is a clown—especially a bull riding event. In the beginning, clowns arrived on the scene as a way to entertain the crowd between shows or events. The role of he rodeo clown has changed since then. Today they are recognized "clowns and bullfighters."

The main reason for the rodeo clown/bullfighters are very often in real danger themselves while trying to save a rodeo cowboy, working to distract the bull so the rider can get to the safety of a rail or a gate. Bulls behave differently than horses. A horse tries to avoid stepping on a thrown cowboy, but a bull will go on the attack at the drop of that cowboy's hat, or anything else for that matter. Also, the bulls used in bullfighting are bred to be smaller, fast on their 2,000 lb. bulk than the ones used in bull riding. They keep competing for years after learning what works and using the strategies to stomp a rider.

One cowboy lamented, "I've been stepped on, swung around like a rag doll and had my face ground into the dirt It's all part of the game. I'd still ride in every rodeo if I could."

RUNNING OF THE BULLS:.

The running of the bulls in Pamplona, Spain was first made famous in Ernest Hemingway's novel, *The Sun Also Rises*. Since then tourists have swarmed to the town of Pamplona, Spain every June to run down the cobbled streets with a herd of angry bulls charging right behind them during "the running of he bulls."

It's also called, "run for your life." The event—part of a festival—begins at 8:00am every morning when 6 bulls are released from their corral near the Plaza, San Domingo. Running in front, beside and sometimes below the bulls, are hundreds of tourists and locals wearing the traditional white outfits with red bandannas.

Not a year goes by without someone getting hurt or killed. Two rockets are fired that signal the bull run has started.

The second rocket means that all of the bulls are running. If you wait for the second rocket you are more likely to be close to the oncoming bulls. If anyone tries to leave the course before the "enciero" (bull-run) is over, they will be shoved back into the same street of the bull-run.

RUSSIAN ROULETTE:

The film, "The Deer Hunter," was a disturbing film about the Vietnam War, even though very few scenes of the war were depicted. It's more about the trauma of war.

One of the film's most disturbing and haunting scenes is when Vietnamese captors place bets on the fate of American soldiers forced to play Russian Roulette, a game of extreme risk, where the player points a gun with only one bullet in the cylinder at his head, and pulls the trigger.

This sport is at the top of the risk scale because it leaves no doubt as to its suicidal intent.

Six people were booked on drugs and weapons charges after a 16 year-old apparently shot and killed himself during a game of Russian Roulette.

Jacob White, of Prairie Ville, Louisiana, and the older friends of his, were playing the high risk game and smoking marijuana when Jacob shot himself. The Ascension Parish Sheriff, Lt. Paul Robert, said that two handguns were passed around the table while they smoked the drug. Jacob White took one of the two guns and loaded it with a live round and put the weapon to his head. As reported in Louisiana's, The Advocate, the gun discharged after the trigger was pulled several times.

PARACHUTING SPORT:

In the world of extreme or high-risk sports, skydiving remains a sought after and popular activity. Deaths do occur, but in comparison to the number of jumps—it's rare. The statistic: one death in every one hundred thousand jumps which reads—30 deaths each year in the United States.

It's reported that skydiving deaths happen the majority of the time due to weather conditions, not parachute failure as generally thought. Although it's true that equipment failure happens in the main parachute, skydivers are required to have reserve—or "back-up" chutes inspected and packed by a certified professional. There are also devices called Automatic Activation

Devices that will activate the spare at a certain altitude if the primary parachute doesn't open.

Studies point to human error and bad weather for the occurrences of skydiver deaths. One of these errors is called "swooping," an advanced maneuver in which a skydiver glides parallel to the ground in process of landing. Strong winds and down drafts are another source of skydiving deaths. Parachutes are caught by changing winds which increase the speed in which the skydiver crashes and dies.

A Brisbane man who died jumping in Norway, wasn't a "crazy guy doing stupid things," a friend defended this extreme sport.

Stephen Richard Ardytan died when his parachute failed to open after jumping off a cliff on Langrabbpiggen mountain, near Sundal on Norway's northwest coast.

The rock climber, BASE jumper and skydiver was jumping with friends, three other Australian and a German man. Stephen was the third Australian in three years to die in BASE jumping incidents in Norway.

In May, 2006, another Queenslander, Tony Cooinbes died when he jumped off Norway's 1,100 meter cliff Trollveggen or "Troll Wall." In July, 2005, Darcy Zoitsas from Adelaide, also lost her life when she was skydiving from the 1,000 meter Kjerag Peak in Western Australia.

BASE is an acronym for: Building, Antennae, Span, and Earth—a rundown of the kind of vantage points from which the sport's participants jump with parachutes.

A Belgian skydiver fell 4,000 meters to her death after a jealous rival disabled her parachute, according to the Belgian police.

Elo Clottemans was charged with murder for causing the death of Els Van Doren. Reported in the London Times, Clottemans was angry with Van Dolren because the older woman was seeing her boyfriend. Police called it a crime of passion.

A pioneer in BASE jumping (jumping from other than aircraft) died in his first jump in decades. Brian Kee Schubert lived most of his life as a policeman in Pomona, California.

Schubert was 66 years-old when he made the fatal jump aat the annual Bridge Day Festival in West Virginia where hundreds of BASE jumpers from around the world met to jump from the New River Gorge Bridge, falling the 876 feet to the water below.

Over 40,000 people, and thousands more watching on television, watched Schubert climb the bridge to applause. Although well known in the sports world, Schubert hadn't been active for decades.

A photographer covering the jump for a local newspaper, Lew Whitener, said Schubert dropped from the bridge but did not open his parachute until he was 25 feet above the water. He died on impact, according according to the emergency personnel at the scene.

Mr. Whitener said the crowd gave a "collective gasp" as Schubert did not open his parachute. A fellow jumper who was standing next to Schubert and getting ready to jump himself, said, "Why Brian didn't open is such a total unknown," adding that the crowd yelled, "Throw! Throw!" urging him to deploy his pilot chute, the smaller parachute that pulls the main sail open.

In October of 2004, a parachutist preparing to jump from a cliff, fell to his death at Tom Sai beach, 390 miles south of Bangkok, Thailand.

Neil Queminet was an experienced jumper from Sudbury, Suffolk, and had been involved in skydiving championships before, and had jumped from skyscrapers.

Neil was with two friends at the Thailand beach resort and had climbed part of the way up the cliff. It was when they stopped to strap into ropes for the remainder of the climb that he fell 100 meters. He suffered head injuries and died from the fall.

A Norwegian parachutist had jumped from some of the world's tallest buildings, had jumped from the World Trade Center, the Empire State Building and the Chrysler Building in New York, the Eiffel Tower in Paris. Thor Axel Kappfjell, 32 years-old, died when he jumped off the 3,300 foot high Kjeraag cliff over the waters of Lysefjord near the city of Stavanger, 300 miles west of Oslo. (Norway)

His body was found near the base of the cliff, his parachute open, police said. It's believed that he probably hit the face of the cliff and slid down.

In March of 2001, at the Carolina Sky Sports, at Louisburg, North Carolina, a videographer who was filming a four-way, exited a twin Otter plane from 13,000 feet

Members of the four-way jump observed the videographer at 2,500 feet with the main bag locked. At the scene the main suspension lines were wrapped around the eye-piece of his camera helmet. The reserve pilot-chute was entangled in the main and the last stow of the reserve was out. The reserve ripcord was pulled and wasn't found. The cutaway release was found near his hand where he died.

The unidentified videographer was visiting from New Hampshire and had made 55 jumps with his camera in the last months.

My own jump-master in skydiving died when her main parachute failed to open, then her reserve-chute also failed to open. She had made over a hundred jumps, and was the one who trained me and four others before we made our first jump.

The bi-plane that I jumped from had gone beyond "the spot," because of my problem of staying on the strut long enough to jump. I was tall and thin, which proved to be a problem—because the plane cruised at 100mph with the motor off—and the wind kept pushing me back into the plane. When the pilot yelled, "It's now or never or you'll be too far from the jump zone!", I shouted to another jumper to "hold me in place so I won't blow back in!" He did—and I jumped.

The "delay" in jumping put us a little beyond the exact spot where I was supposed to jump and land. I remember being excited about my parachute opening, (and grateful) and the free-floating sensation before gravity level. As I hovered near earth, though, I could tell that I was in trouble. I was headed right into some trees. To avoid that disaster, I redirected the "chute" by pulling on the parachute lines. I drifted past the tops of the trees and breathed a sigh of relief until I saw that I was about to land in the middle of a golf course while people were on the green—playing golf.

I landed hard, fell back on my helmet, and took off like a rocket because the device that releases the harness was stuck. I passed several golfers while trying to release it. What—rather who—rescued my obvious peril, was a guy I was dating at the time. Steve saw that the plane had drifted past the jump zone, saw me almost land in some trees, and saw what was about to happen, (golf course) and took off in his jeep to save the day. Remarkable as what he did sounds, it's really what happened. He ran out onto the golf course just as I was zooming by and he grabbed my jump boot—thankfully not the one that I badly sprained when I hit the ground.

It was probably a good thing that I sprained my ankle and was "grounded," because there was an organization of stunt-skydivers that asked me to join them that summer. Last I heard, he was still jumping at the same skydiving club in Decatur, Texas.

WING WALKERS:

Wing-walkers. What—or who—are they? They are those daredevils who entertain air-show crowds by walking the wings of a bi-plane—without a parachute—and in flight!

Back in the barnstorming days of the 1920's and '30's, almost every aerial act featured a "wing-walker" or two, with pilots sometimes doubling as walker.

Today, you can count the number of nationally touring wing-walkers on one hand, and still have a couple of fingers left over.

This is a story about Cliff Winters. He was known as one of the "crazy" jumpers in the late '50's and early '60's. He began his career in the Army in the 82nd Airborne. It was during this time that he became a wing-walker, and made jumps for a flying circus.

Cliff Winters opened parachute schools at Santa Ana, California, and in Hemet, CA. The Hemet drop zone was later bought out by Parachutes Incorporated. Cliff also did stunts for the movies—crashes, wing—walking, and daredevil stunts.

At the Labor Day Air Show at Chino, California, 1963, Winters snap-rolled a special Ryan with a double wing into the ground and was killed.

HANG-GLIDING SPORT:

During a world series competition in Australia, a pilot in one of the hang-gliders fell 1,500 meters to his death. His parachute failed to open after the flying pod separated from his hang-glider in mid-air.

"He attempted to activate an emergency parachute, which appears to havae malfunctioned, and he plummeted about 5,000 feet to the ground where he died instantly." said Sgt. Steve Howard.

About 80 hang-gliders were competing at the Forbes Flatlanads Championships in January of 2007. Represented were 57 international pilots from 17 nations.

"The competition has been put on hold and the people I've spoken to were quite upset about losing a colleague in these circumstances," Sgt. Howard said. He added that they were all aware that hang-gliding is a very high-risk sport.

HOT AIR BALLOONING:

A well experienced hot-air balloonist, Chris Marshall, who had competed in several world championships died in a crash.

He was taking a group of tourists on a hot air balloon safari over the Masai Mara natural game reserve in Kenya when the aircraft crashed. At around 6:00am, witnesses said the balloon's burner seemed to have gone out only briefly after the hot-air balloon took off.

Balloon safaries are taking off for anyone who can afford it. It's a popular adventure for tourists who want to see Africa's wild animals roaming about in their natural habitat.

But is it risky? The founder and chairman of Balloon Safari, Ltd, Alan Root, said that it was the second crash in a month.

CLIMBING MT. EVEREST:

Climbing is a popular sport, but high altitude climbing is more of a high-risk challenge because of the constant threat of losing your life.

This particular challenge mentally became a research study by different teams who examined how climbers prepared physically as well as mentally to succeed at reaching the top of the mountain.

High altitude climbing as an extreme sport has many enthusiasts from all over the world. But the sport requires a rigorous strategy of preparation just to survive to make it to the top, which separates the men from the boys in adventure with the risk, not suicidal intent.

The high altitude alone, according to Bahrkeo Shukitt Hale takes its toll on the climber's energy and resources, both mental and physical. Lassitude, weakness, breathlessness, the slowing of thought and acion are he main effects, he explained. Adding, exposure to avalanches and extreme conditions of weather. And there may be other challenges, like fatigue, loss of focus, or resolve to go on.

Research indicates that statistically there are similarities between Olympic performance outcome and particular mental skills among top-notch athletes. Shared factors contributing to success were found to be these: quality preparation, training, setting clear goals, imagery, simulation training, mental preparation for competitions, and on-going learning.

To add to that list, top athletes had well-developed skills in managing stress, concentration, motivation, courage and confidence, and being fully prepared.

Evidence obtained from the study on high altitude climbing and mental preparation indicates principles involved for excellence. For example, researchers Terry Orlick reports that there are seven decisive elements that direct the pursuit of high level performance on a consistent basics: commitment, focused connection, confidence, positive images, mental readiness, control of distractions, and ongoing learning.

Ever since Sir Edmund Hillary and Tenzing Norguays made the first successful climb to the top of the world's highest mountain, 8,843 meters, in 1953, others have taken on the challenge in ever increasing numbers.

However, only a small per-cent actually reach the summit. Egan (2001) reports that over 300 climbers attempting the climb died trying. Reasons given for the failure include: loss of will to continue, loss of focus, high altitude sickness, injury, fatigue, and extreme weather conditions.

With death factored in as a close participant or a serious injury researchers are of the definite opinion that to undertake such an extreme sport, with high altitude climbing a prime example, the athlete must have tremendous physical stamina and mental strength to be successful.

They further describe that detailed planning and imagery help off-set or entirely eliminate problems that might come up during the climb. A high priority is mental toughness. The individual has to be able to endure emotional discomfort and keep going.

The study suggest that the desire and the ability to focus on the task in front of you, combined with a strong mind-set are essential in order to make it.

Relatively few have succeeded in reaching the summit of Mt. Everest. These elete were highly skilled at focusing on doing the right thing at the right time on the mountain. This type of mind-set helps you to achieve the goal in spite of problems.

The element of focus included getting into a zone, breathing and monitoring their pace, concentrating on the priority of directing mental and physical energy to immediate task. Their focus was very engaged on the orderly process. The act of focusing enables the climber go get rid of distractions, concentrate and follow through on the objectives on an in-the-moment clarity of purpose throughout the day.

Included in the study were statements from climbers. One said, "Very few times on Everest would I ever let emotions in . . . . At base camp you could, but not on the mountain. There was too much responsibility for yourself and others. You had to stay focused. I stick to the task at hand—that is my motto."

A strategy that helped the climbers, too, was setting short-term goals that aid in staying focused and committed to the main goal—which was not just reaching the summit, but coming back down alive.

"Some climbers put their goals in the wrong place. They put it on the top of the mountain. You should really make your ultimate goal to come back to base camp. It's important also to set little goals along the way," offered another climber.

For another it was the accumulation of experience and the lessons learned from the failures and hardships that proved to be the most valuable tools in venturing to climb Everest.

Chapter Ten

Not The Final Chapter:
A Better Way—Not An Ending

Radical Psychological Moods Dark Fall—Bipolar and Unstable Minds and Suicide, is meant to be a direct parallel to "the (dark) Fall of Man."

There is a direct link, in my opinion, to creation (not evolution) of mankind in perfect balance in Genesis, before pride and vanities, and the dark downfall of man into degeneration.

Apart from God a human being is standing on precarious ground. Human nature is the cause of man's descent. Another way of putting it is, mankind's nature is to sin . . .

"Sin, says Christianity, is inherent in man's nature. Unless something is done to destroy the power of sin in the heart of man, his existence in a scientific world will always remain under the shadow of imminent self-destruction."—Charles Clayton Morrison, in The Christian Century, March 13, 1946.

In that realm of spiritual degeneration where sin procreates sin and death, man is desperate and self-seeking. There's a continual disintegration and decaying of the body and soul—that is repugnant to life-force before sin. In that state, man irrationally seeks to return to dust and readiness, to await another turn of the Potter's wheel.

Suicide, to me, is the futility of a life without meaning, wrongly pushed to judgment by a fallen nature that's rejected God.

Because God loves us, He sent His son, Jesus Christ, to step into that world of degenerate sin and death. Christ died on the cross and took on all sin to give us a bridge—a way to be re-born and regenerated into eternal life.

The answer to "a better way—not an ending" and the riddle of suicide, can be found in a simple belief and a "re-birth into light and hope, love and purpose," where lies and destructive forces have no power. That transforming life, out of despair and endless dark fall, is found in the Bible. A prominent scripture is, "For God so loved the world, that He gave His only begotten son, that whosoever believeth on Him should not perish, but have everlasting life. John 3:16.

Giving your life to God to become a new creation is a good beginning to new life. You'll be out of the clutches of self-destruction and death. This is a choice, and is there for you as it was for me.

There are new beginnings and ways to get there. The rest of this "better way" chapter is putting together an accessible network of people to contact, places to go to find what you need.

"Feelings" can delude you, keep you in a hopeless, depressed state. One decision, one action, can make a difference, and these positive reinforcements will reassure you as you gain confidence.

First things first, of course, and the most immediate call for help in a life—or-death situation is either "911," or Suicide Crisis Hotline. An operator can connect to the "Suicide Crisis" number. (Resources are also listed at the back of this book.)

Interventions can be information and education, medication at a hospital emergency room by doctors, a phone call to a crisis number, or talking to a friend, family member or clergy. These are emergency measures and needed, but a focus on mental, and emotional and spiritual needs is crucial for change and overcoming.

(poem)   "Perhaps everything terrible is—
          In its deepest being,
          Something helpless
          That wants help from us."
                              (unknown author)

IF YOU ARE IN CRISIS AND NEED SOMEONE TO TALK TO OR NEED IMMEDIATE HELP, PLEASE CALL 911.

- SUICIDE HOTLINE—1-800-784-2433
- DOMESTIC VIOLENCE HOTLINE—1-800-799 (SAFE) 7233

A myth about suicide is that if a person "talks about suicide—they won't attempt it." If a person expresses an intent to take their own life, take them seriously and help them find mental health resources and treatment. What is true is that very depressed people may not be a good judge of whether or not they need help, or even how to go about finding that help.

SUICIDE PREVENTION PROGRAMS:

The first suicide prevention telephone hotlines were established by mental health professionals in the 1950's. The lines are staffed 24/7 by counselors or trained volunteers.

Today, more schools are providing suicide-prevention programs that give training for students and teachers, and school staff to recognize warning signs and tell them where to refer students at risk for suicide.

SUICIDE PREVENTION (SUPRE)

The problems:

> In the year 2000, approximately one million people died from suicide: a "global" mortality rate of 16 per 100,000, or one death every 40 seconds.

> In the last 45 years suicide rates have increased by 60% worldwide. Suicide is now among the three leading causes of death among those aged 15-44 years (both sexes); these figures do not include suicide attempts up to 20 times more frequent than completed suicide.

> Suicide worldwide is estimated to represent 1.8% of the total global burden of disease in 1998, and 2.4% in countries with market and former socialist economies in 2020.

> Although traditionally suicide rates have been highest among the male elderly, rates among young people have been increasing to such an extent that they are now the group at highest risk in a third of countries, in both developed and developing countries

> Mental disorders (particularly depression and substance abuse) are associated with more than 90% of all cases of suicide; however, suicide results from many complex sociocultural factors and situations (e.g. loss of a loved one, employment)

Interventions That Work:

> Strategies involving restriction of access to common methods of suicide have proved to be effective in reducing suicide rates; however, there is a need to adapt multi-sectoral approaches involving other levels of intervention and activites, such as crisis centers.
> There is compelling evidence indicating that adwequate prevention and treatment of depression, alcohol and substanace abuse can reduce suicide rates.
> School-based interventions involving crisis management, self-esteem enhancement and the development of coping skills and healthy decision making have been demonstraed to reduce the risk of suicide among the young.

The challenge is that, worldwide, the prevention of suicide hasn't been discussed primarily because of a lack of awareness of suicide. It needs to be brought out into the light and talked about openly inside and outside the mental health sector. A comprehensive, intensive approach, that includes education, religion, law, police, labor, politics and the media.

There are consequences to what we believe. Our beliefs can lead to steps we take in life that can help or harm us. That includes what we believe about ourselves and why?

In life there is suffering, and introspection is difficult. Even if we reveal a flaw, that doesn't mean we accept or acknowledge the truth about ourselves. If we've become accustomed to our ways we have to want to change or we may rebel angrily at ourselves to defend our ego.

> "I have seen all the works that
> are done under the sun; and behold,
> all is vanity, a striving after wind and
> feeding on the wind."
>
> Ecclesiastes 1: 14
> . . . all is vanity and vexation of spirit.

If we live in denial of the dark side of our fallen nature, we reject and refuse to accept the human sin "beingness" that needs salvation. As we accept this human condition we find ourselves in, we can by faith be transformed.

RESOURCES

1. Nationwide Crisis Hotline Numbers: 1-800-333 4444 or—1-800-799(SAFE)7233.
2. National Rape Crisis Center (that will connect you to a center in your area. 1-800-HOPE
3. Domestic Violence Hotline: 1-800-799-7233
4. American Association of Suiciodology—*http:www.suicidology.org*
5. American Foundation for Suicide Prevention—http:/www.afsp.org
6. National Organization for People of Color against Suicide—http:/www.geocities.comnopcas
7. National Alliance for the Mentally Ill—http:/www.nami.org
8. Suicide Prevention Advocacy Network—http:/www.spanusa.org
9. Suicide Awareness/Voices of Education—http:/www.save.org
10. 1-800-SUICIDE—http:/www.hopeline.com

www.ingramcontent.com/pod-product-compliance
Lightning Source LLC
Chambersburg PA
CBHW051432280526
45785CB00003B/1262